A Foundation Course for
Language Teachers

CAMBRIDGE LANGUAGE TEACHING LIBRARY

A series of authoritative books on subjects of central importance
for all language teachers.

In this series:

A Foundation Course for Language Teachers

Tom McArthur

1983

Cambridge University Press

Cambridge

London   New York   New Rochelle

Melbourne   Sydney

Published by the Press Syndicate of the University of Cambridge
The Pitt Building, Trumpington Street, Cambridge CB2 1RP
32 East 57th Street, New York, NY 10022, USA
296 Beaconsfield Parade, Middle Park, Melbourne 3206, Australia

First published 1983

Printed in Great Britain by the University Press, Cambridge

Library of Congress catalogue card number: 83–7416

British Library cataloguing in publication data
McArthur, Tom
A foundation course for language teachers.
1. Languages, Modern – Study and teaching
I. Title
418′.007   PB36
ISBN 0 521 25279 2 hard covers
ISBN 0 521 27271 8 paperback

UP

To David Abercrombie –
for many reasons

Contents

Acknowledgements

Firstly, I would like to acknowledge a considerable debt to David Abercrombie, David Crystal and William Littlewood for their help at important points in the preparation of this material for publication. Their informed critical comment was invaluable.

Secondly, many colleagues, students and friends have also played a significant part in the development of this book. Among colleagues and friends I would like particularly to thank Judith Cowan, Jean-Paul de Chezet, Catherine Devillers, Robert Dole, Agnes Drever, Marie-Claire Dugas, Patricia Gordon, Harinder Marjara, Feri McArthur, Ronald Sheen, and Meinrad Staudigl. Among students, important help was provided by Judy Bougaieff, Paul-André Deshaies, France Jutras, Elizabeth-Anne Malischewski, Aglaja Schnitter, and Germain Veilleux.

Additionally, I would like to take this opportunity to express my warm personal appreciation, for many reasons not unrelated to this book, to the organizers of SPEAQ: La Société pour la promotion de l'enseignement de l'anglais, langue seconde, au Québec, in particular to Josette Beaulieu, Joan Boeckner, and Patricia Foy for their professionalism, their support and their interest. If the future lies with organizations like SPEAQ, then it will be an interesting and stimulating future.

Finally, I would like to express special thanks to Adrian du Plessis of Cambridge University Press, for his humane encouragement and expertise in seeing this book safely into print; and to Kay McKechnie for her professionalism and care in copy-editing the typescript.

It is something of a cliché to say that the virtues of a book are largely due to the help of others and that the sins of omission and commission are very much one's own; there is often, however, a hard core of truth in clichés.

Introduction

This book is for both practising and potential language teachers. It can be used for university and college training courses, for refresher courses and summer institutes, and for private reading. Its content has developed over the past fifteen years, first at the University of Edinburgh, then at the University of Quebec. My own experience as a language teacher (in Scotland, England, India and Canada) has been largely but not entirely with English as a second language; the material discussed here, however, relates to language teaching and learning generally, whether the target language is labelled 'first', 'second', 'third', 'foreign', 'living', or 'dead'.

Ours is an age of information overkill: it is increasingly difficult to keep up to date as more and more material is published relating to such subjects as applied linguistics, classroom techniques, visual aids, and the latest methodological revolution. For some of us, this steady bombardment of information is depressing; for others, to go shopping in the rich new supermarket of the publishers is a stimulating challenge.

Whatever our response, however, this state of affairs appears likely to stay with us for some time. It is the climate in which the next generation of language teachers will learn their trade. My concern here is to help equip them as effectively as possible to survive and succeed in that climate.

A Foundation Course for Language Teachers deals with three themes that have persistently recurred in my own career and that seem nowadays to be constants in the lives of language teachers:

1 the increasing influence of linguistic science on language teaching, and the need for teachers to have as clear as possible an appreciation of what linguistics is and is not, and what linguistics can and cannot do for us;
2 the perennial question of grammar, of what we should know, think and do about it both as a concept with a long and complex history and as a controversial element in our everyday work;
3 the need to have coherent strategies for handling the pressures exerted upon language teachers by educational systems, by our own and our students' needs and hopes, and (importantly) by the impression of constant turmoil, change and uncertainty in methodology.

The three distinct but interrelated parts of this book are attempts to survey these issues. Written primarily for student teachers, they are as direct and non-technical as possible, while seeking to avoid over-simplifications that would misrepresent the complex issues under discussion.

Part 1 Linguists and language: some basic principles is a survey of what linguists seem generally able to agree about, or disagree least about, coloured however by my own emphases and by certain basic assumptions and concepts which I hope will make themselves clear as the book proceeds. One such assumption is that an awareness on our part of what linguists disagree *least* about will serve as a basis for further study of what they disagree *most* about.

Part 2 Twenty-five centuries of grammar: an examination of our cultural conditioning is a historical and social review of how we acquired and how we respond to the concept 'grammar', along with a consideration of both the debt that we owe to our predecessors and the need to be wary of the patterns of expectation that our heritage has imposed upon us. Again, the review can serve as a foundation for further study, and as a core around which students can formulate their own policies about the place of grammar in their work.

Part 3 The gift of tongues? – A review of language teaching in its sociocultural setting is a consideration of choice (and lack of choice) in language learning, as well as the methods and approaches currently competing for the attention of language teachers, the whole discussed in relation to our educational systems and general cultural attitudes towards language, language teaching and language learning. At various points I offer my own suggestions as regards various well-known dilemmas and ideological stances, but ultimately the reader is left to make up his or her own mind about the matters discussed.

The three parts are supplemented by three appendices: the first describes ways in which the book can be used in courses, the second lists review questions linked to the parts and sections of the book, and the third provides a range of possible topics for projects, term papers and discussions, also tied in with the parts and sections. These in turn are followed by notes and references, a select bibliography, and a general index.

There is no painless way for students to develop their professional skills or for practising teachers to perfect their craft. There can, however, be more effective ways of acquiring the necessary fundamentals for one's career than may have been available in the past in a somewhat fragmented and often disputatious profession. This book is a contribution towards that goal.

1   Let no one tell you again that science is only for specialists; it is not. It is no different from history or good talk or reading a novel; some people do it better and some worse; some make a life's work of it; but it is within the reach of everybody.
(Jacob Bronowski,
A Sense of the Future, 1977, p. 4)

---

2   Actually, thinking is most mysterious, and by far the greatest light upon it that we have is thrown by the study of language. This study shows that the forms of a person's thoughts are controlled by inexorable laws of pattern of which he is unconscious. These patterns are the unperceived intricate systematizations of his own language – shown readily enough by a candid comparison and contrast with other languages, especially those of a different linguistic family.
(Benjamin Lee Whorf,
Language, Thought and Reality, 1956, p. 252)

---

3   By speech we design great bridges and fight wars, we express our deep feelings and our spiritual aspirations, and even set forth our most subtle linguistic theories. We can talk, we can talk about talk, we can talk about talk about talk, and so on forever. Language is the special treasure of our race. It depends on what we call the mind, but it comes out of the entire person. To learn a second language is to move from one mystery to another.
(Earl Stevick
Memory, Meaning and Method, 1976, p. 3)

Part 1 Linguists and language: some basic principles

A survey of what linguists seem generally able to agree about, or disagree least about, coloured however by my own emphases and by certain basic assumptions and concepts which I hope will make themselves clear as the book proceeds.

At first glance, linguistic theory of our time seems to offer a stunning variety and disparity of clashing doctrines. Like any age of innovative experimentation, the present stage of reflections on language has been marked by intensive contentions and tumultuous controversies. Yet a careful, unprejudiced examination of all these sectarian creeds and vehement polemics reveals an essentially monolithic whole behind the striking divergences in terms, slogans, and technical contrivances.
(Roman Jakobson,
Main Trends in the Science of Language, 1973, p. 12)

1.0 Introduction

Modern civilization owes much to the development, over the last five centuries, of 'the scientific method'. This method of examining, classifying, theorizing and testing was first of all applied to the study of natural forces and substances (in physics and chemistry), then to the study of life forms (in biology, physiology, etc.) and more recently to human nature and social organization (in anthropology, sociology, psychology, etc.). Scientific attempts to understand the phenomenon of language are, however, more recent still – although serious interest in the structure and use of languages goes back more than two thousand years, and such studies were often (in civilizations such as ancient Greece and India) highly systematic.

Language is central to our natures as human beings, yet it seems that we had to examine almost everything else 'scientifically' before we could embark on a reasonably objective examination of how we communicate and think.

There is, however, at least one good reason for this. Language is a social artifact – a tool. People who use tools do not generally spend much time studying them. Instead, they *use* their tools to create other things.

4

Occasionally, a carpenter will buy or even invent a new tool, but few carpenters will take the time to create a theory of tools – even though such a thing might eventually revolutionize both tool-making and tool-using. In the same way we have tended to make use of our faculty of language without trying to analyse it objectively. In brief, we have taken it for granted.

Our lives increasingly depend, these days, on fast and successful communication, and when discussing the many social ills of our society we often attribute them – wholly or in part – to poor interpersonal communication. Ours is an era when even machines are 'learning' to use language, and we have to come to terms with its *realities*, as opposed to easy traditional *assumptions* about what it is. At the beginning of this century, the Swiss linguist Ferdinand de Saussure observed, as regards language:

Il serait inadmissible que son étude restât l'affaire de quelques
spécialistes; en fait, tout le monde s'en occupe peu ou prou;
mais – conséquence paradoxale de l'intérêt qui s'y attache – il
n'y a pas de domaine où aient germé plus d'idées absurdes, de
préjugés, de mirages, de fictions.
    (*Cours de linguistique générale*, 1916/1978, pp. 21–2)

(It would be unacceptable for its study to remain the concern of
only a few specialists; in fact, everybody is more or less involved
in it, but – and this is the paradoxical result of the interest that
attaches to it – there is no subject more prey to absurd ideas,
prejudices, fantasies and fictions.)

Linguistics is currently at a stage similar to early physics or biology, a time in which a variety of more or less competing hypotheses and systems of description have not yet given way to one agreed view. A basis of 'received knowledge' agreed by a majority of linguists is only now emerging, while a consensus about the terminology to use is still some way off in the future. Apart from the fact that linguistics is simply too recent to be a unified science, there are at least four other reasons why the area continues to present problems to linguist and layman alike:

1 Human language has shown itself to be an exceedingly complex phenomenon, far more so than most educated people appreciate at present.
2 Unlike other sciences, which use language to handle *something else*, linguistics has to use language to describe language, which is a very demanding exercise. (We have no means of getting outside language in order to examine it better. It is like trying to remove one's skin in order to see how it works.)
3 Language is by its very nature beyond the total grasp of any one human or group of humans. It extends from the past through the present into the future, and it extends across millions of users who

will never communicate directly with each other, even where they share what is regarded as 'the same language'.

4 Language, like thought, is both a private and a shared phenomenon, and until we understand the reality behind such terms as 'the brain' and 'the mind' we will only have an appreciation of the product rather than how it is produced, stored, memorized, used as part of 'consciousness', and so on.

It is not surprising, therefore, that the research, argumentation, claims and counter-claims of linguists may appear strange, irritating or even absurd to outsiders – and even less surprising that many persons concerned professionally with language – such as writers, translators, teachers, critics, littérateurs, traditional grammarians and lexicographers, journalists, etc. – should have mixed feelings about the development of linguistics. Many such persons have felt that, in an area of aesthetics and sensitivity, the 'pseudo-scientist' is just not welcome to intrude. They have also resented the new ambiguity infused into the word 'linguist', as well as the (apparent or real) arrogance of certain schools of linguistics whose less mature adherents have acclaimed certain ideas with messianic fervour.

New movements such as linguistics and ecology are always in danger of becoming fashionable. People jump on the new bandwagon and expect or claim too much too soon. They thereby join the interested parties mentioned by de Saussure, with their prejudices, fantasies and fictions.

The objective study of language, however, has proceeded steadily, and even at this early stage in its development has produced a range of interesting propositions which – like developments in physics and chemistry in the past – have certain important consequences for all of us.

1.1 A science of language

Although there are natural historical connections between modern linguistics and older forms of language study, there are certain fundamental differences between the two.

The science of linguistics has been in existence since about the beginning of the twentieth century. It developed in the main out of the nineteenth-century scholarly study best known as 'comparative philology', in which materials from different languages and historical periods were studied and compared as texts and parts of texts. It also has a strong link with the traditional study of grammar and rhetoric, and a good argument can be made for an unbroken line of development from the language studies of ancient Greece and India through Latin, Arab and Western European scholarship to the present day.

The main differences between modern linguistics and the long-established scholarly studies of language are:

1 Linguistics does not depend upon a traditional 'mythology' of any kind to support its conclusions or bias the direction which any investigation might take. The ancient Greek Stoics, for example, studied language because they believed that the Greek of their time (fifth century BC) was corrupt, and they wanted to find the *étyma* or 'true forms' from which the language had degenerated. Again, many students of language in the eighteenth century believed that all languages descended from ancient Hebrew, citing the Biblical story of the Tower of Babel as proof. Elements of these and other myth-centred approaches to language are still quite common.
  (I am not using the words 'mythology' or 'myth-centred' here in a pejorative sense, but in the sense of a set of values, beliefs and supporting quasi-historical stories which condition mental attitudes. It can be argued seriously that 'science' is just part of a more recent mythology, in which case linguistics might well be less different from the older views than we suppose. Certainly, it relates to a scientific theory of 'reality', and the line between theories and myths is not always sharp and clear.)

2 As a science, linguistics is supposed to be an objective, descriptive and predictive activity, and its findings should be subject to confirmation or disconfirmation by means of properly conducted tests. Previous approaches to language have not been like this, and are generally subjective and prescriptive (or normative). The belief that a god, for example, chose one particular language as his medium of revelation, or that one's own language is the most satisfactory for logical thought are both unlikely to allow objective analysis to take place.

3 As a modern academic activity, linguistics tends to be relativistic; that is, it functions on the assumption that values, judgements, theories, etc., all vary according to such things as time, place, environment, background, inclination and – especially – culture. There is therefore a tendency to be wary of dogma, and even where its own assertions begin to look dogmatic a mature student will try to avoid absolutism. Statements about language within the field of linguistics can therefore be taken as inherently provisional.

4 Linguistics is an autonomous study, whereas earlier language disciplines have tended to exist because of some pre-existing need. In ancient India, the Hindu brahmins became experts in the phonetics of Sanskrit so that they could recite the sacred Vedas more accurately and pass them on orally with less chance of corrupting their purity. In Europe the study of Latin grammar was linked with such things as

veneration for a vanished civilization (Rome), enthusiasm for a particular form of religion (Roman Catholicism), and assumptions about the kind of training that was best for young members of certain ruling élites. Most people still tend to believe that the study of one or more languages is related to the improvement of a person's ability to perform. Linguistics has nothing directly to do with such things. It may study them, among other human activities, but it makes no advance claims in the area of, say, improving language teaching and learning. This is a point which is often misunderstood, partly because in the years following the Second World War many people in the United States proposed a 'linguistic approach' to language teaching, and also because many people today talk about 'applied linguistics' as a kind of cure-all for the traditional 'faults' of language-teaching methodology. Any benefits which emerge from linguistics in *any* area (whether teaching or computer technology or lexicography or whatever) are very desirable, but they are not the essential *raison d'être* of linguistics, any more than the marketing of a new medical drug is a *raison d'être* for biology or chemistry.

5 As a science, linguistics is concerned with *all* aspects of language equally, and not, for example, only with sacred scriptures, literary masterpieces, printed texts or standard dialects. To pursue such general concerns, it therefore aims to be as exhaustive, as consistent and as economical as possible in whatever theories and descriptions it might at any time set up.

The foregoing is a description of the ideal but does, I think, cover a great deal of what actually goes on under the name of 'linguistics'. There are, however, a variety of distinct schools or movements with their own special traditions, terminologies and emphases and it can take a student a number of years of careful study to come to terms with this *embarras de richesses*.

Over the past few years I have slowly attempted to list the essential principles that a majority of linguists throughout the world would today agree upon as an area of common ground. The list is a subjective selection made after some fifteen years of reading and discussion, and presently stands at twenty principles which could probably have been expressed in a variety of alternative forms, with equal effect. The important point is, however, that the bulk of them will be found recurring in the majority of general manuals on the subject, but not necessarily with my emphases.

1.2   Language-using animals

Linguists see language as a defining characteristic of being human. In their view, we are therefore 'language-using animals'.

One of the problems of using language to discuss language is the need to be clear – constantly – as to what one intends by a particular word. The above statement depends – crucially – on whether we can agree about the meanings of 'language', 'human' and 'animals'. In discussions with students at various times I have had problems with all of these, many persons wishing – for various reasons, but often because of strong personal involvement – to insist that certain animals *do* have languages, or that human beings are *not* animals.

In the wide sense of language as a 'signalling system' certain of our co-habitants of earth do have languages: apes, dolphins and bees for sure. In the narrow sense of 'system with creative potential in thought and communication', however, we do seem – as far as present knowledge indicates – to be the only users of this particular tool. It might be sensible, though, at this stage, to propose that the gulf between the least fluent human and the most communicative animal is part of a continuum rather than a line separating the human box from all other boxes for communication among living organisms. We will meet this kind of problem of 'continuums' and 'containers' throughout this study.

Let us propose then that human communicative ability – that is, language *per se* – is the most complex and creative of such abilities at present known on this planet, and is at one end of a continuum, with the signalling systems of the less complex animals at the other end. The abilities of birds, bees, dolphins and apes would therefore come at various points on the continuum, each having its describable list of advantages and disadvantages.

No known human community fails to have a language, and all known languages are complex structures. Every one of them, however, shares an arresting common aspect which is ignored by and large because it is so 'obvious': the human race everywhere shares a common heritage of vocal–aural apparatus. Equipment that was originally intended and used for eating, drinking and breathing (mouth, nose, throat, lungs, etc.) and for the general reception of certain vibrations in the air (the ear) has been brought into an intimate relationship of a *secondary* kind, and all the richness of language springs from this ingenious adaptation.

Most people educated in the Western tradition probably nowadays accept the fossil record, the idea of geological time, and the biological theory of evolution developed in the early nineteenth century by Darwin and Wallace. Not all do, however, and for many such persons the description of human beings as 'animals' is at its best wrong and at its worst an insult. For such people there is a sharp dividing line between humanity and the other creatures living on this planet, and the fact of language may well be used to help strengthen the argument that human beings are a special creation by a particular god. If, however, one takes the word 'animal' in the sense of a complex living and moving organism with a structure of cells, a cycle from birth to death and some kind of social behaviour, then our own form of life can be linked with these other forms. Linguists generally would appear to accept the evidence of palaeobiology and comparative anatomy as well as the theory of evolution in its current form, and take the view that 'language' is a particular kind of tool developed millennia ago by our ancestors at the same time as they developed more obvious tools like sharpened sticks and skin bags. It was also a powerful force for social cohesion, while the development of dissimilar languages among dissimilar groups was probably also a powerful force for mutual suspicion and hostility: two sides of the same coin.

1.3 Acquiring a language

All normal human beings, under normal conditions, are born with the capacity to acquire at least one language, and probably more than one.

The first problem with this principle is the need to agree on what we mean by the word 'normal'. This, again, is a very relativistic and culture-bound term, and psychologists have traditionally pointed out that it is far easier to establish *ab*normalities than forms and behaviour that follow a norm.

Crudely, however, we can assume that human infants without birth problems of a serious kind or defects passed on genetically, fed and loved and introduced into society in ways which most of us would consider usual, do learn to talk and to listen, responding intelligently to what they hear. The crucial activity is done before the child reaches its fourth year, and most children are well launched into their first language(s) by the time they are five, which means that

1 the child has made one of its greatest mental efforts – possibly the greatest single success story of its life – before it is fully aware of itself as a personality capable of thought and effort;
2 everything contributing towards this achievement has been done before a systematic memory has been established;
3 all of the patterning has been laid down, in effect, as an unconscious or at the very most semiconscious procedure of a largely spontaneous kind.

If science were actively searching for a recurring human miracle, then this process of language acquisition would make an excellent candidate.

It is only when the child enters the more artificial confines of school that it is asked to reflect upon the language it uses, and this is by no means easy. It is rather like asking someone who has learned to ride a bicycle to think about how he or she does it, the kind of self-conscious activity that could lead to falling off. Yet our civilization insists that children combine the unconscious art of language with fresh, fully conscious language arts like reading, writing and grammar. In addition, the activities of schooling increase through the years around ten, when the brain is moving towards a more adult form and the old spontaneous learning skills are weakening. All language learning that follows these years is much harder, more conscious and far less spontaneous than what happened in childhood.

I would argue that the learning of a first language inhibits the acquisition of other later languages, mildly in some cases, massively in others, yet at the same time all over the world people acquire two, three or more languages to varying degrees of competence, at various times in their lives. No means exists at present of measuring the effort required for such achievements, or of finding out how the brain handles the 'extra' load.

Bilingualism is a much debated matter, but – as is the case with so many other things – analysis of the problem depends to a great extent on how we define the word 'language'. Suppose, for example, that a child acquires Language A from one source and Language B from another. The child becomes efficient with both, but is not really aware that it is bilingual; it is simply learning language. At some stage an appreciation develops that two distinct systems are involved, and that many people cannot handle both, but in a world that could handle both, would the two systems still be regarded as distinct languages? Similarly, a person who is bilingual between Dutch and German is not bilingual in the same way as between German and Chinese, where the systems are so different. Again, if a child is brought up to handle two or three variants of the same language (as I was, in Scotland), is that child still only unilingual, or bilingual, or trilingual, or what? Normally, the answers to these questions are provided from social consensus, not in purely linguistic terms. (We are actually back once again with the question of containers and continuums. When does one language such as Dutch become by slow gradation across frontiers another language such as Flemish or German?)

The cardinal question nowadays about child language acquisition, however, relates to basic human nature: is the skill essentially programmed genetically, or is it learned socially – or, indeed, is it a combination of both? The general assumption today is that every human child has an innate disposition towards language and possibly even some 'wiring' as regards certain universal elements in language, but that just what particular form develops will depend on the unique social events that surround the child. Such is the balance of nature (heredity) and nurture (environment).

1.4 Individuals and language

This capacity to acquire a language or languages does not, however, mean that all human beings can use it or them with equal facility.

The constellation of genetic and environmental factors makes each human approach to language unique. In a real sense, our concept of 'language' is a social abstraction from the actual capacities of unnumbered individuals each different from the other. No two humans perform linguistically in the same way. To put it in an interesting but extreme form, each of us is the sole native-user of our own private language. Technically this individual achievement is called one's 'idiolect', and that idiolect is the sum-total of all a person's language experience and performance to date.

Social and political ideas over the last century at least have been strongly coloured by the idea of human equality, that in some sense all of us are created equal. Linguistics cannot support the naive assumption that we are – or should be seen as – all equally capable. Such a viewpoint might be best kept for such concepts as 'all equal before the law' or 'all should have equal social opportunity'. There is little doubt that in language terms, as in physical skills, mathematics and art, some individuals have egregious talent, others are variously deficient, while the great mass of persons have a fair capacity to handle language. Linguistic science cannot currently offer any serious hope that everybody can be provided with a 'flair' for learning foreign languages.

At the same time, however, there is reason to suppose that many of us are cleverer than we think at language acquisition. Adequate motivation is a powerful factor in any kind of language learning, and many social groups and educational systems implicitly or explicitly influence people into accepting less from themselves than they are capable of producing. Massively unilingual communities often militate against second-language acquisition, because the society implicitly does not believe in the worthwhileness of any other language. Societies which expect conformity of one kind or another may also quietly persuade their members against a whole range of intellectual and social adventures, language learning among them.

The history of the teaching or learning of foreign languages is complex, but essentially seems to divide into two kinds:
1 the 'marketplace' tradition, where other languages are acquired for purposes of trade and are only learned to the immediate level needed for such contact. This kind of activity has often in the past led to 'interlanguages' (often called 'pidgins') between the languages of two groups, usually (in crude general terms) with the vocabulary of one language linked to the grammatical system of the other. Many speech forms that are now respectable national tongues began life in this fashion.

2 the 'monastery' tradition, where originally a language was learned for
a specific cultural – usually religious – reason, in special austere
colleges, and generally limited to the young men of certain socially
important groups (élites): monks, priests, civil servants, officers, etc.

As the idea of general education developed, especially in Western Europe
after the Reformation, school and college education was widened, and the
learning of the 'classical' languages, Latin and Greek, was supplemented
with the study of one or more non-native literary traditions. Only very
recently in human history have educational institutions seriously sought to
provide their students with an everyday conversational mastery of a second
language.

Additionally, we have today in the state educational systems of most
modern nations a tension between the traditions of market and monastery,
between the idea of a 'vocational' and 'practical' education towards a 'job',
and the rival idea of a 'cultural' and 'literary' training. This tension is not
anywhere near resolved as yet, and it influences the process of second-
language learning profoundly. It relates to social and political policy, and
linguistics can only play an advisory or observational role in such matters.

I share the view, also, that a knowledge of the basic assumptions of
linguistics can serve to clarify our attitudes to language, and that policy-
makers may in future be able to understand their problems and needs better
if they have an appreciation of what language is and is not. This is probably
what de Saussure meant when he said that the subject should not be
confined just to a few specialists.

1.5 Signals, symbols and emotions

*Every language is a system of arbitrary signals and symbols. We invest
considerable emotion, however, in such systems.*

This principle points to a central paradox in language. The noises and marks
on paper of a language could be any noises or any marks as long as they
made sense as a whole to the group of people involved. Whether an animal
is called 'a pig' or 'un cochon' or 'un puerco' or 'ein Schwein' makes
no difference at all to the animal, but a great deal of difference to the human
being wanting to talk about it. All four of these 'words' for an animal are
equally good or equally bad as a means of labelling it. They work, first of
all, because everybody can see that certain animals with certain qualities
are sufficiently of one kind to merit one label – and, secondly, because over
centuries of history certain groups of people have settled upon certain noises
and marks on paper to represent the generic nature of those animals.

This is hard for many people to grasp. There is no God-given reason
why in English a pig should be 'a pig'. There are sound historical reasons,
which most people are not interested in, and these reasons explain the

feeling of rightness that people have about the name and the animal. For an English-user, therefore, 'pig' is always seen as the primary and somehow 'right' label for the animal, and 'cochon' or 'puerco' or 'Schwein' a way of encoding it into a secondary system for handling reality. It is hard to persuade children in general and often adults too that a foreign language is just as primary as one's own language – to *its* users.

This is where the emotion comes in. The system of one's native language may be arbitrary, but the amount of social effort and significance invested in it is so great that for most people it is part of themselves, inseparable from their sense of identity, their image of self. Erwin Schrödinger, one of the world's leading physicists and winner of the Nobel prize in 1933, said of this indissoluble tie with the first language that one learns: 'The difficulties of language are not negligible. One's native speech is a closely fitting garment, and one never feels quite at ease when it is not immediately available and has to be replaced by another' (preface to *What is Life?*, 1944).

If Schrödinger felt this, then how much more the general speaker of German or English or French or whatever? The evidence throughout the world of language riots and strong opposition to the imposition of one language upon another – the whole idea in Canada of 'the two solitudes' that are English and French – indicate that despite the fact that a so-called language is simply patterned noise or marks on paper, we human beings become passionately involved or monumentally biassed when questions of language preference arise.

One advantage of a linguistic approach to language is that it encourages a second way of looking at one's native language as well as at all other languages. This second way is characterized by the idea of 'distance': one seeks to distance oneself, at least while doing linguistic work, from the ordinary everyday emotional pressures of being a user of Language A or Language B. This does not mean that a person would want to risk psychological trouble by trying to achieve an unreal objectivity, but rather that for certain purposes and on certain occasions an element of dispassion can be obtained, or at least striven for.

1.6 Languages and worldviews

The language that we learn as children places certain constraints on the way in which we interpret and organize the world in our minds. This is part of our 'mental set' or worldview, and relates to what is technically known as the 'weak' Sapir–Whorf Hypothesis.

Edward Sapir and Benjamin Lee Whorf were two American anthropologists-cum-linguists who, in the first half of this century, studied language in general and North American Indian languages and societies in particular.

They found that such Amerindians as the Hopi of Arizona have such different conceptions of reality from people of European origin that 'translation' between their views of reality and ours is extremely difficult. Their speculations have come to be known as the Sapir–Whorf Hypothesis. In its 'strong' form, this hypothesis suggests that a meeting of minds between such alien cultures is impossible; in its 'weak' form, it suggests that a meeting of minds is simply hard work. Most linguists today follow some version of the 'weak' form.

It is fairly easily demonstrated. The commonest demonstration relates to light and colour. Science talks about a spectrum of light similar to the rainbow, but it requires language in order to cut this spectrum up into specific colours. Different groups determine their primary colours differently, even when they come from relatively similar backgrounds. The British linguist John Lyons makes the following observation as regards two European languages:

(T)here is no equivalent to (the English colour) *blue* in
Russian – the words *goluboj* and *sinij* (usually translated as 'light
blue' and 'dark blue', respectively), refer to what are in Russian
distinct colours, not different shades of the same colour, as their
translation into English might suggest.
   (*Introduction to Theoretical Linguistics*, 1968, pp. 56–7)

Consider the problem of the Russian translator of an English-language novel in which there appears the phrase 'a blue dress'. How should it be translated? No help is given in the English text, because the writer could never have foreseen the problem.

The problem becomes more severe as languages increase in cultural as well as geographical distance from each other. The American anthropologist Stephen Tyler notes:

Not only do cultures differ among one another in their
organization of material phenomena, they differ as well in the
kinds of material phenomena they organize. The people of
different cultures may not recognize the same kinds of material
phenomena as relevant, even though from an outsider's point of
view the same material phenomena may be present in every case.
For example, we distinguish (in English) between dew, fog, ice,
and snow, but the Koyas of South India do not. They call all of
these *mancu*. Even though they can perceive the differences
among these if asked to do so, these differences are not
significant to them. On the other hand, they recognize and name
at least seven different kinds of bamboo, six more than I am
accustomed to distinguish.
   (Introduction to *Cognitive Anthropology*, 1969, pp. 3–4)

An analogy may be useful here. To find positions on a map (and by implication on the surface of the earth, somewhere) a cartographer draws in latitudinal and longitudinal lines, numbering each line, and in this way creates a grid. Where he starts is arbitrary and does not matter – as long as other cartographers and map-users agree to accept his conventions. His grid will do its work very well, even taking into account the curvature of the earth, but it is not The One True Grid – and, more significant still, there are no such lines on the surface of the planet earth.

Similarly with language. Each language places its grid upon our sense impressions (and so by implication on the world *out there* beyond our eyes and ears). In this way it makes reference, interpretation and communication possible. Its words are, as it were, numbered grid references, arbitrarily placed upon the world-map, each useful in terms of the others around it, functioning well enough because, over generations, its users have been in rough agreement about it. But the grid imposed by one language differs in innumerable tiny ways from the grid imposed by another. Technically speaking, they are seldom isomorphic. Some languages are closer together, some further apart. One would expect, for example, a greater congruency between Swedish and German, say, than between Swedish and Tagalog, Tarahumara or Telugu.

The cartographer, however, in reality has a far easier job, for maps are simpler than languages. Firstly, languages change slowly with time. Secondly, they vary slightly over distances, from community to community; and, thirdly, every user is unique. It is as if our map grid slowly adjusted its lines *all the time*, so slowly that generally one did not see this happening, while, in any case, it looked different to every single user. With a map two people can hope to find exactly the same spot on the surface of the earth. With a language, they have to settle for approximations. Cartography could not survive the conditions governing language.

Yet this is what the child learns, what comes in time to fit as close as the skin: the native language with its corresponding view of reality. One defence of second-language teaching, different from purely economic or cultural defences, is the psychological one, that the foreign language constantly reminds the learner that other grids exist.

1.7 The medium and the message

Our appreciation of how language is used includes both the medium and the message: how something is communicated as well as what is being communicated.

Essentially, the *message* is what a person wants to say about his or her circumstances, some event or whatever, while the *medium* is the linguistic substance and system by means of which the message is conveyed. The process is analogous to an electric current (the message) and the wiring (the medium). The two are so closely linked that they are often taken to be the same thing, to such an extent that the Canadian educator Marshall McLuhan has said that in modern life 'the medium *is* the message', that is, *how* something is presented is the essential factor rather than its content. There is social cynicism here, in the view that the packaging has become more important than the contents, but the important thing for a study of linguistics is that the two elements of communication should be clearly recognized as separate.

The French linguist André Martinet recognizes the distinction as primary and secondary articulation, the two aspects of what he calls 'double articulation'. Primary articulation is what I am calling the message; it is informative. Secondary articulation is what I am calling the medium; it is a kind of vehicle. Double articulation, this duality of organization, is true of all languages everywhere. The odd thing is that one can have the medium without the message, but one cannot have a message – ever – without its medium. That is, it is possible to produce (and comedians sometimes do it) a string of nonsense syllables distinctly English or French or whatever, but the creation of a disembodied message is impossible (without, say, some kind of telepathy).

1.8 Sounds and surfaces

In technical terms, there are two major mediums of language: the phonic medium and the graphic medium.

Quite often, when linguists discuss language, they deal only with the phonic medium, that is, with organized human vocal sound and how it is interpreted by the ear. Certainly, this medium is primary in a historical sense: it came first in the history of the human race; it also comes first in the language acquisition of every child. This fact should not, however, obscure the fundamental point that in principle a whole variety of mediums are possible: sound (as we use it); marks on surfaces, to be understood visually (as we do with ordinary writing and print); marks on surfaces, to be understood tactilely (as we do with Braille script for the blind); pure gesture (as we do in the sign language for the deaf); light (as used in heliographic signalling); and, theoretically, even more exotic procedures such as systems of physical pressure, odours (similar to pheromones among insects), danced movements in three dimensions (like the 'language' of bees) and so on, indefinitely.

Originally, human language was uniquely sound-based (with peripheral gestural aids), but with the development of our kind of civilization there came the revolutionary transfer of the message to a secondary medium: writing. Although it was originally derivative, this second medium immediately proceeded to obey its own rules, and there is no necessary one-to-one correlation between the phonic medium (of sound) and the graphic medium (of writing). Each has advantages and disadvantages in relation to the other. Sound, for example, is more spontaneous and (until the advent of recording apparatus) transient, whereas writing is usually carefully contrived and relatively more permanent. Both, however, share one crucial quality of all language mediums: they are linear, either strings of sounds or strings of letters. Language involves length and time, and uses these two as its only means of making comments upon the fluctuating world of length, breadth, height, depth, colour, time, transience, etc.

It is possible to imagine a language existing only in the graphic medium (that is, without a system of pronunciation). Latin in Europe and Sanskrit in India have come quite close to this fate, as so-called 'dead languages'. It can also be said that the ideograms of classical Mandarin Chinese have no real spoken form, any more than, say, the number 5 (also an ideogram) has a true spoken form. Like the pig, it is one thing in one language, something else in another. Written numbers are, in fact, a means of communication between persons who do not share a common language, as are the pictograms now popular for such things as international road signs.

1.9   Verbal and non-verbal communication

How we handle the phonic medium (that is, how we learn to speak) creates our 'articulatory set', and this particular cast of mouth and jaw, etc. (typical, by and large, of our whole speech community) conditions not only how we speak our native language but also how we will attempt to speak our next language. In addition, the articulatory set is linked with such other socioculturally significant matters as 'body language', 'personal space' and 'social distance'.

The idea of the *articulatory set* might best be described as like a person's handwriting. It is obvious to most of us that everyone has a unique 'hand', but at the same time that it is usually (in part at least) shaped by the style of handwriting popular in a community when the child learned to write. There are various national styles of handwriting, as there are styles in accent.

The articulatory set is the product of every effort the individual has made since babyhood to conform to the language behaviour of those around it. Working by ear and eye, the child has correlated the movements and positions of the mouth with millimetric precision, by trial and error and repetition, by inference, induction and classification, until it achieves the right kind of tension of the muscles, shape of the lips, use of the tongue and breath, and so on, to qualify it as a genuine member of a speech community. This is a major act of conformity, and its very success means that flexibility is to that extent restricted when the time comes to attempt the articulation of a second language – or even an alternative accent of the first language. The variety of accents in the world testifies to the permutations possible within the limited space of the mouth, nose and throat, all of great delicacy but also great tenacity once established.

This fact helps us to understand why the teaching of pronunciation is so difficult a business, and also suggests that a holistic approach to pronunciation, where the total positioning of mouth, tongue, etc., are considered, might serve us better in future than an atomistic approach to individual speech sounds in the second language.

The articulatory set does not operate in a vacuum. It has intimate links with the whole face, the eyes, how the head is held, neck and shoulder movements and so on, until we find that it is part of what is now called *body language*. The positions of parts of the body, stance, gestures and such things are individual matters, but they are also in part culturally conditioned and in part universal. They assist the phonic medium, and function regardless of whether they are being seen or not, as can be verified by watching someone talking to an unseen and unseeing listener on the telephone. They are absent, of course, in the graphic medium and this in part contributes to the impersonal quality of the written word.

As if this were not enough, body language is linked to yet another social, cultural and communicative element – *personal space* and *social distance*. The phonic medium together with gestures and the like needs a field within which to operate, and individuals have certain preferences as to how far they should be from others while communicating, and how often they should look directly at those others or be directly looked at in return. This again varies from society to society, but can be an important factor in the social side of language learning. When one learns a foreign language in the company of its users, one usually also learns foreign body positions and, ultimately, becomes aware – whether consciously or unconsciously – of the norms operating among users of that language as regards space and contact.

These matters are now being studied systematically, and technical terms for body language are 'kinesics' and 'paralanguage', while some investigators refer to the study of social distance and personal space as 'proxemics'.

One salient feature that has emerged from all such studies is the essentially un- or semiconscious nature of language performance, articulation, body language and social positioning. Innumerable processes are involved, a multitude of signals are sent and received, and the bulk of them occur at a level which is below the threshold of what we call 'consciousness'. In fact, the less conscious one is of the procedure, the more competent one is. Consciousness is, on many occasions, a hindrance rather than a help, and the essence of second-language acquisition would appear to be, as many have suggested, the passage of the student as rapidly and as painlessly as possible from conscious effort to other-than-conscious skill in the medium and its supplementary activities. The medium would appear to be most effective when it obtrudes least in the communication of the message.

1.10 Languages 'fuzzy at the edges'

Languages are not mutually exclusive, either in social terms or in the head of the bilingual person. Interpenetration is inescapable.

Down the centuries many pleas have been made for the retention of the 'purity' of a language, often with the assumption (like the Stoics in ancient Greece) that there was an earlier and better time, somewhere, when the language *was* used purely by everybody. Additionally, many purists have looked to the written literary form as in some sense the means of transmission of a language in its most desirable state, perhaps because the element of greater permanence in the graphic medium encourages the idea of stability.

If languages were indeed containers (that is, if there were a kind of sociohistorical box labelled 'French' and another labelled 'English' and so on), then some case might be made for sealing any holes that might allow the transfer of material from neighbouring boxes into the particular box to be defended. This description is of course a metaphor, and it is sometimes useful to treat languages *as if* they were boxes, but there does not seem to be any real sense in which any language can be regarded as separate and distinct from any other. Languages appear to be (to use another metaphor) 'fuzzy at the edges', and if they were to be described in terms of mathematical set theory then they would be overlapping sets, not distinct entities. In other words, languages such as French and English, for example, for all sorts of historical reasons are in a permanent state of intermixture, slowly giving and taking as they adapt through time.

Individual attitudes to, say, Anglicisms in French or Americanisms in British English may vary in relation to particular social and political problems, and such attitudes may well have effects upon the *degree* of interpenetration that occurs at any time or in any place – but such attitudes do not affect the massive natural fact of interpenetration. If two language communities meet at any point, then along the line of contact there will be interpermeability. If any individual is going to use the two languages, then within that individual's head there is going to be interpenetration (or, positively, cross-fertilization; negatively, contamination). Various kinds of 'interlanguage' will inevitably arise.

1.11   Equal potential among languages

All languages are equally capable of expressing whatever their users need them to express, and have equal potential, although historical events may significantly benefit or impede a particular language.

One often hears or reads that certain languages are 'better' for certain things, while certain other languages are more musical, more masculine or feminine, more aggressive, sweeter and so on than others. These are all subjective suppositions, and such assertions are worthy of study; they should not be dismissed out of hand, but at the same time they are not necessarily true. They may simply represent the hopes and biases of certain people.

It is certainly true, however, that a language does best what its users in any period or place have wanted it to do. In the nineteenth century, for example, English and French had detailed vocabularies for describing horses and carriages, much of which is no longer generally needed, while some has passed on into the later vocabulary of automobiles. The Inuit or Eskimo are famous for their capacity to describe Arctic conditions and animals, while the Arabs are equally renowned for their language's coverage of desert conditions and life. At a particular time in its history a language may, therefore, be strong in one area but weak in another. This, however, can change if its users want it to change, either (1) by importing the necessary expressions directly from another language, (2) by translating foreign terms into new native expressions, or (3) simply by creatively expanding the systems that they already have. Languages can also change their very structures drastically over time. The English language, for example, changed over 1,500 years from a highly inflected structure (Anglo-Saxon or Old English) to the loose analytical style of today, so that one can seriously ask whether these are really still the same language.

1.12   Flux

No language is static. All languages are dynamic, capable of description along the lines of diachrony and synchrony.

All languages are in a constant state of flux, and the larger the community of speakers, the greater the flux. As we have seen, conservative persons tend to regard the changes through time as degeneration, while innovators may regard them as progressive. It is probably safer to follow the example of Edward Sapir and say that languages *drift* in time and that the direction of the drift can, to some extent, be mapped. At the same time, we can observe the attitudes of users towards the various changes, including our own attitudes.

Ferdinand de Saussure introduced the opposition of *diachrony* and *synchrony* into the description of language. A diachronic development is 'through time', while a synchronic state is 'across space at a particular time'. The relationship is often compared to the length (diachrony) and width (synchrony) of the trunk of a tree, and is shown axially as:

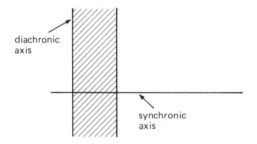

Many linguists in recent decades have preferred to engage in synchronic analyses of language, often ignoring the historical dimension completely, as a consequence offering us a quasi-static view of language phenomena. Others, in the past, favoured history at the expense of contemporary description. I endorse the view that such biases have led to imbalance, and would argue strongly that we are most usefully served by taking both axes of description into account.

1.13 Diversity

No language is homogeneous. All languages are by their nature heterogeneous. All individuals have their idiolects, while communities have their accents and dialects, and at some point these shade into recognized languages. The idea of a standard language is the product of civilization. The standardization of any language is an artificial social and educational activity, built on to the essential diversity within any language group.

There is a tendency among many people to believe that if a language is *not* homogeneous then it ought to be, that it is somehow less respectable as a language. This attitude leads to a strong advocacy of the standard form (if there is one), a preference for the certainties of the written form (if they can be clearly tabulated), and an attitude which infuses words like 'dialect' and 'patois' with pejorative overtones.

This is all the more remarkable because diversity in a language is a constantly observable fact, and most people admit freely that one region, city, class, book or whatever may have a monopoly on prestige. Most languages have prestige forms (for all purposes or for certain purposes, pursuits and people), and the prestige form is often regarded as the actual 'proper' (and therefore only legitimate) form of the language. Arabs will dismiss their everyday colloquial forms in favour of the classical Arabic of the Koran; Greeks extol the virtues of the language of education, Katharévousa, but actually speak Demotikí; the French tend to favour the middle-class speech of the Ile de France linked with the written norms of the language and certain educational traditions; the people of England regard Received Pronunciation (RP) or 'Queen's English' as the best way to pronounce the language, although only a small minority among them actually speak it that way.

The favoured forms, which are also usually the standard forms (but not always), are generally a minority usage, and this minority is usually linked with a higher social position. No linguist could, however, ignore the other varieties of the language and concentrate only on the prestige forms if he or she wished to be a serious and comprehensive student of that language. Additionally, the teacher of a language – while concentrating on the standard form as provided in his or her textbooks – also needs to be aware of what a student will actually meet in the streets and homes of the target people. Otherwise, a great deal of frustration follows from learning one version of a language and then discovering that very few people use it and even that, in certain places for certain reasons, that form is disliked, or has at least important social overtones which the student was never told about.

Because standard forms of a language are so powerful – in education, government, broadcasting and the like – it is very easy to forget that they are historically *secondary* to the continuum of dialects that spreads across nations and often does not stop at frontiers. Modern communications appear to have strengthened standard forms, but do not seem to have had much effect in making people change their local forms of speech. The written language is generally far more homogeneous than the spoken form, but this homogeneity arises very much from the fact that different dialect groups interpret the common script in their own terms. The script, of course, is accent-free, giving no particular value to the signs for vowel and consonant, but the moment someone interprets those signs into speech we return to diversity and divergence – if not disagreement and disapproval.

People are often quite savage towards other people's idiolects and dialects. A knowledge of language reality may, one day, contribute towards a reduction of tension and social unease in this area, people being less willing to criticize and more willing to accept – and even enjoy and experiment with – the range of options available within a language or across languages.

None of the above is an argument against standardization. Standards develop as part of a socializing process in nation-states which link themselves with a 'national' language (although languages as such are not inherently national). One advantage is ease of communication, but this ease does not require total conformity. Most nations, such as the United States and the United Kingdom, manage well enough with modification towards a relaxed norm, and most people have a tendency anyway to make small adjustments when in contact with people from a distance, speakers of other dialects. This does not mean that, when at home and at ease, they need maintain the national or supranational norm: they can go on using the local forms, which are usually emotionally important in a person's sense of self, and visitors may well be invited to learn some of these, facilitating their sense of involvement in the new milieu.

1.14   The politics of language

The line between one language and another is often drawn for political and cultural reasons, rather than for linguistic reasons.

In a free situation, with a need to communicate somehow, people will use any combination of signs, noises, pictures and the like. In Europe or in India people regularly draw upon all and any language resources they may have to 'get by'. In Yugoslavia and Turkey, for example, I have shamelessly put together pieces of English, French, German, Italian and Greek in order to get somewhere. Consider, similarly, the history of the human race, especially in its ports, pilgrim centres and crossroad cities. At such places all the world met, and had to communicate. Away from such contact points scholars and pedants might dream of purity of race and language, but *need* is a stern realist, and languages are the products of need long before they are affected by legislation.

It is safe, therefore, to assume that where there is a defined community speaking Language A and another defined community speaking Language B not far away, then at Point C where they meet there will be miscegenation. If, additionally, there has been historical tension between these groups, then a whole Area C may at various times be under the domination of A or B. Alsace, battleground between the French and Germans, is a good case in point. Montreal, a trading point of contact between the North American speakers of French and English, is another such case. In such places, there is a linguistic tug-o'-war between A and B.

Conversely, if communities with related 'dialects' split into distinct nations, the dialects are often then elevated into distinct 'languages'. This is the case with the countries of the Scandinavian peninsula, the Iberian peninsula, and Western Europe from Belgium and the Netherlands through the Germanies to Switzerland and Austria, with all sorts of attitudes towards what a language is or isn't. 'Dutch' and 'Flemish' are seen as languages, but 'Low German' and 'Schweitzer-Deutsch' are not, while Austrians simply speak 'Austrian German'. The Portuguese deliberately made their language as different as possible from Castilian Spanish, but their close cousins in Galicia (inside Spain) are not entirely free to regard Gallego as a language, and have to learn Castilian all the same.

Countries which are semi-independent within larger states end up with 'semi-languages': in Scotland 'Scots', with its own literature, is regarded by some as a distinct language, by others as only a special dialect of English; in Spain, the Catalans have difficulty establishing their language as a separate thing from Castilian Spanish, although everyone knows that these two are as far apart as standard Spanish and standard Italian. I can read Spanish; I cannot read Catalan. Most speakers of English cannot understand Scots.

No matter how firm and clear a language appears to be, it seems that there are always fuzzy edges, zones of indeterminacy. 'English' seems very much an entity, yet a case can be made that a lot of it is mutilated French, and that academic English is a creole of Neo-Latin. Cicero and Caesar, if they could overhear a university seminar in English, might have the same feelings that anglophones have when they encounter Melanesian Pidgin English. 'French' seems a very definite language, but how does the 'langue d'oïl' in the north relate to the 'langue d'oc' in the south, to the very different languages Basque and Breton, to Provençal, to Alsatian and to the forms of Belgium, Switzerland, Quebec and the francophone enclaves of North America, to *la Francophonie* in Africa and Asia? In the south of France Occitan and Catalan meet, dividing 'real' French from 'real' Spanish – and what about the historical argument that modern French is only one form of Latin, that so-called 'dead language'? What was Latin anyway? The forms used by the Catholic Church or taught as classical ('golden') Latin were not what the everyday citizens of the Roman Empire used. We do not know much about what *they* used, and it is *their* Latin that became the Romance languages.

It is not, therefore, so much a question of neatly labelled containers, each with its national language, as a question of continuums through time and across space. A language teacher has, of course, to provide a neat container of material for students to learn (in the sub-containers of books and units and so on), but that same teacher risks much when he or she fails to remember that a language cannot be put into a box and the lid closed upon it. Political and social decisions and attitudes, however, create the illusion that just this has been done for most of the respectable languages of the world today.

1.15   Making models of language

Language and languages can be described according to models, some better,
some worse, all provisional – convenient fictions which should not be
promoted to the status of absolutes.

A 'model', as proposed here, is essentially a description, in the same way
that a map, diagram, silhouette, plan or normal scale model is descriptive.
Models are pragmatic tools, and are not normally claimed as absolute or
comprehensive. Following the recommendations of the Austrian philosopher
of science Karl Popper, we can say that a hypothesis about something is
a creative act, an educated guess on the basis of available evidence and the
ability to see patterns – and that the models that emerge from theorizing
will relate to specific goals, will function well or badly in relation to those
goals, can be replaced in due course by better models based on more
satisfactory theories, and are therefore by nature provisional. They are *not*
what they describe, and should not be confused with it. They are analogues
of a limited kind, created for our practical convenience.

This short philosophical excursion is necessary to establish that a
'grammar' of a 'language' is just such a model. Created by human
observers of human language, a grammatical description asserts that the
language behaves in certain ways. It therefore claims to be predictive, but
no known grammar actually succeeds in predicting all the possibilities in
a living language. Indeed, some authorities have suggested that the very
success of Pāṇini's ancient grammar of Sanskrit in Hindu India delineated
the language so rigorously that it contributed towards the demise of
Sanskrit as a living language. It became instead a static kind of language
game for brahmins to play. Classical Latin is in a somewhat similar position,
being also a pretty well closed system based on certain canonical texts.
There is, and can be, no further input into such languages. A really
successful grammatical description of a language, thoroughly applied by
teachers and firmly supported by a legislating academy, could well weaken
the dynamism of that language by denying various assumed exceptions
and attempted extensions (variant syntactic structures, new words, new
senses of words, etc.). Practical grammars and dictionaries do not normally,
however, have the power to 'fix' any living language; rather, they follow
on behind it as it develops, cataloguing its activities.

Models and descriptions are enormously useful – as long as their
relativistic and pragmatic natures are appreciated. No representation which
says 'language is like this' should be asked to support more weight of 'truth'
than its frame can reasonably bear, and any such frame will be largely
dictated by our reasons for creating it. Thus, 'English for medical purposes'
is at first sight a manageable area, and (various provisos made) a model can

be set up which would allow materials to be developed, say, for the teaching of this kind of English to foreign students of medicine. General grammars and language descriptions work in just such a way, even when they are being put forward as definitive, comprehensive, and final. They cannot, however, in the very nature of things be either definitive or comprehensive or final.

I have already in this survey offered a simple model of language: that it consists of *medium* and *message*. This can be expressed diagrammatically in two ways, as:

or as:

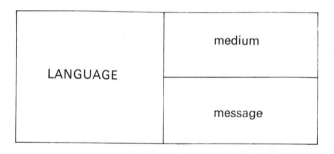

This latter presentation is no better or worse in general terms than the first, but serves to show that model-making, descriptions, taxonomies, etc., are in essence container-making activities. Little boxes, like these, are useful, as long as they are seen to be procedural devices, and not facts of life.

The above model can be extended as follows:

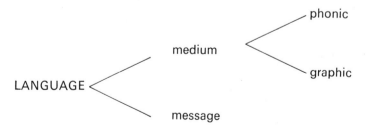

This says quite a lot, clearly and succinctly, and with notes and explanations the model could become quite complex and useful. It is, technically, a two-level model (medium and message) and will take us quite far, but it differs in a number of important ways from an alternative three-level model that is widely used by linguists:

	phonology
LANGUAGE	syntax
	semantics

This model foregrounds the phonic medium (as phonology) and ignores the graphic medium. It also implies that syntax or grammatical organization serves as a kind of link, bridge or mediator between sound on the one side and meaning on the other. This works well enough as far as it goes, and it is, by and large, the most popular current model, whereby linguists and language teachers can, for example, talk about 'the phonology, syntax and semantics of Language X', and in this way cover a great deal of useful ground. There is, however, a great deal more to any language than these three handy containers suggest.

As a lexicologist, I would like to know where the lexis or lexicon or word-store or vocabulary (call it what you will) goes in such a model. Is it part of the syntax or part of the semantics, or should a fourth level be created to give it a place of its own? If such a level were added, where would it go, and would it spoil the neat suggestion of syntax as a bridge? Some theorists more or less ignore this question, others seek to accommodate lexis in various ways, but however the models are constructed and reconstructed none of them, even the most efficient, does more than hint at the complexities involved. Hints, however, can be useful things, can help create an awareness of the problems involved in language description, and may even lead to a decent humility in the inquirer.

1.16 Conservation versus innovation

Languages are simultaneously conservative and innovative. Languages taken together with the social attitudes and assumptions of their users (whether conservative, radical, purist, perfectionist, laissez-faire or whatever) are studied in the branch of linguistics called 'sociolinguistics'.

In each language there appears to exist a dynamic tension between conservation and adaptation, reflecting society as a whole. These opposing tendencies relate to a whole gamut of attitudes among its users as regards such things as: social levels of formality and informality, colloquial and literary, standard and regional, personal and impersonal, respectable and vulgar/taboo, proper and slang, correct and incorrect, refined or barbarous, current or archaic, and so on. This vast area is also subject to the problem of containers and continuums, insofar as some things may be very easily put in a box labelled 'formal language', whereas others may be 'more or less formal', or 'formal under certain conditions', or 'formal for some people but not for others'. I have used the category *formal* to make my point, but one can use any of the others listed with it to achieve the same end: 'more or less taboo', 'personal under certain conditions', 'barbarous for some people but not for others', and the like.

The findings of sociolinguistics (the sociology of language) are often of great natural interest to language teachers, translators and other professionals, because they deal with social factors that strongly affect what one does. Thus, for example, a tendency towards greater informality in the United States has had its effect on the teaching of English in Quebec and on the way in which certain short forms are used by Quebecers in speech and writing rather than the more usual long forms. Because of their wide use as colloquialisms in language courses, forms like *don't* and *I'd* are used in formal and informal writing alike, the user in Quebec being largely unaware of any qualitative distinction between, say, *I don't* and *I do not*.

1.17   Language, mind and brain

Languages and the processes of thought are intimately linked. It is probable that the two abilities developed together. When linguistics moves into the area of psychology it is known as 'psycholinguistics', and when it moves into the area of neurology it is known as 'neurolinguistics'.

Language is a product of many things, but ultimately it derives from the electrochemical activity of the brain. A study of language – as opposed to languages or a particular language – leads inevitably to questions about the nature of consciousness and unconsciousness, memory, storage, retrieval and the like. In an age when the computer is becoming so important, the human brain is often compared to a computer (or vice-versa), and a shared terminology of 'input' and 'output', 'software' and 'hardware', 'circuits' and 'wiring', etc., has developed for both. Like all such analogies or metaphors, a parallelism like this reveals much, but may also serve to conceal other equally important factors. The brain–mind totality may resemble a computer (and vice-versa), but it is *not* a computer as such. It is a brain, and one of the odder things in our odd world is that today the brain is engaged in studying the brain, just as linguists are using language to study language. At present, however, we are only on the threshold of the discoveries to be made in neurology, psychology and linguistics as regards this vast inner terrain. As a consequence, the hybrid studies nowadays known as 'psycholinguistics' and 'neurolinguistics' are still in their infancy.

Throughout the discussion of these various principles of linguistics we have been on the edge of a discussion about 'reality' and how the mind or brain or mind–brain conceives and manages 'reality'. Over the ages we have shaped our languages and they in turn have helped shape us, in a vast inextricable and largely unrecorded process, where a person's language and very sense of self become hostages to fortune. The language skills resident in our mind–brains are closer to us than our very skins, and their detailed on-going investigation demands in turn great skill and caution. We are so sensitive about our languages that tomorrow's psychoneurologists and computer enthusiasts alike will need to tread softly in telling us both what we are like, there, inside our heads, and what analogues can be set up out of metal and plastic to match us, word for word and sentence for sentence.

1.18 Language in its contexts

Any expression of language is bound by time and space. It relates to a linguistic, a situational and a sociocultural context. Any item of language also, usually, co-occurs with other items, and these make up its co-text (whether spoken or written). Items of language in total isolation have no function; they need a system and a setting to give them both function and meaning.

Children often ask for the meaning of a word in isolation, without seeing the need to provide any setting for it; too quick and too casual a reply can often have unexpected consequences, as for example when the child asks what 'cricket' is and you say it is a game, and then discover that it was '*a* cricket' in the context of insects. Even if we know the strict linguistic context we may need to check further, into the situation beyond the language and even into the society and culture beyond that, to be sure of just what the item of language is supposed to be doing. The line between a dictionary interest in a word and an encyclopaedic or general-knowledge interest can be difficult to establish, as in the following sentences, each with the item *man* omitted:

1 I saw an old _____ sitting under a tree.
2 In biological terms, _____ is an animal.
3 The captain told them to _____ the boats.
4 The men were in one boat, and the women _____ned the other.

5 No _____ is an island (John Donne).
6 _____ is an island between Britain and Ireland.

The fact that there *is* an island called Man may be considered by some as purely fortuitous, providing us with a homonymous placename that is not in any serious sense to be linked with the everyday item 'man'. Perhaps, but placenames have to be spoken aloud too. One foreign learner hearing 'Man is an island' and little else might very justifiably be as confused as another hearing for the first time the famous quotation 'No man is an island'. Meanwhile, for feminists the idea of women 'manning' a boat may be anathema, but the sentence is perfectly possible; the system of English permits it.

We often work with words, knowing their contexts ourselves but failing to reveal those contexts sufficiently to others, and are surprised when we are not understood. Similarly, dictionaries often provide definitions of words in the form of several rough synonyms, without providing any context at all, whether linguistic, situational or sociocultural. Hopeful users may then put the 'right' word in the 'wrong' place, or fail to understand a word as used in a particular context. An increasing number of wordbooks, however, drawing upon linguistic research, try in a variety of ways to avoid this problem of decontextualization, especially by providing style labels and examples of usage wherever possible. Their compilers are very much aware that few, if any, true synonyms exist and that, as John Lyons has observed, such things as synonymy are largely 'context-dependent'.

1.19   Success and failure in communicating

Language is generally described as a means of communication, but in studying it we constantly come up against the question of what it is to be 'competent' in communicating.

'Competence' is a central issue in linguistics, whether in terms of abstract syntactic theory (as with Noam Chomsky) or in terms of social interaction (as with Dell Hymes). What it all boils down to, however, is the question of how and whether we 'get it right' when we seek to transmit a message to someone else. We communicate, but our communication has no guarantee of success, and the feedback we get from the words and actions of others often indicates that they have received something (subtly or massively) different from what we thought we were transmitting.

In the early decades of modern linguistics (with Leonard Bloomfield, for example, in the 1930s), research and speculation were more with structure and system than with meaning and language-in-the-world. In the 1950s, particularly under the influence of Noam Chomsky, attention moved from external analysis and the establishment of units of language to questions of an ideal native speaker–hearer's ability to perform, and the underlying competence that made this ability possible. Nowadays, prompted by Dell Hymes, there is a strong concern for the social reality of language and the nature not just of systemic competence but of 'communicative competence', how people manage to use language for what they want and need. There is a darker side to all this, however, which (as I see it) has yet to be adequately confronted: the issue of 'communicative *in*competence', the problem that our efforts at interacting are characterized as much by failure as by success.

When people teach a second language, they often behave as though the students are (or should be) thorough successes in their *first* languages. Do we have any firm reason for supposing, however, that anyone is completely consistently competent in any language, or is it rather that our languages and our abilities with them are inherently approximative, matters of more-or-less rather than yes-and-no? Study of the brain in recent years indicates that language relates directly only to a small part of our complex personalities; the limitations upon success with language may well become central issues in tomorrow's linguistics, once some idea of the basic structures and systems that we use has been achieved.

Socio-, psycho- and neurolinguistics may one day contribute forcefully to our general education, in that they will be able to tell us much more than we currently know about the intermeshing of language and worldview (in terms of individuals, groups, cultures, and the species at large), and about how we can best seek to acclimatize ourselves one to another. A complex technological civilization appears to demand a far greater effort at sympathetic communication than earlier tribal or even national pre-industrial societies. A degree of what one might call 'sociolinguistic compromise' may be part of more successful communication: taking time to bring differing worldviews more into line (without immediately feeling hypocritical, disloyal, or whatever) – an updating of the old but useful adage about 'trying to see the other fellow's point of view'. Major and minor fanaticisms often interfere with the process of acclimatizing or even our willingness to consider the possibility. Even where people do take the time to acclimatize to others, situational stress and emotion may prevent balanced communication, as areas of the brain take over which deal in basic reflexes of survival rather than the delicacy of present-day social adjustment.

'Therapeutic linguistics', however, does not yet exist, and I cannot assert here that everything I have said in the last paragraph is consciously part of the general consensus among linguists today. There are, nevertheless, in the concern for questions of ethnicity, class and language use, sexism and nonsexism, and the like (detectable in various recent publications, and conferences), indications that people working within the ambit of linguistics are increasingly aware of the need to address themselves to questions of success, failure, adjustment and satisfaction in the business of using language socially.

1.20   An outline history of modern linguistics

Modern linguistic science is the result of the coming together of various traditions and schools. Some knowledge of the origins and diversity of these traditions and schools can help us both understand the often conflicting terminologies used, and appreciate the common direction in which most of the schools are nowadays moving.

As indicated at the start of this review, linguistics is a relatively recent science with, however, venerable connections. Its nature and these connections can be described in a variety of ways, but here one simple three-part diagram may be sufficient in order to exhibit a historical trend:

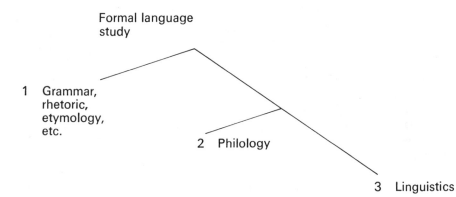

1 *Grammar, rhetoric, etymology, etc.*, dating from Greco-Roman times, writing–centred, prescriptive, and linked with such things as the art of composition, the study of literature and the arts/humanities, traditional logic, and philosophy.
2 *Philology*, dating from the late eighteenth century, diachronic, descriptive and comparative, and incorporating etymology from (1).
3 *Linguistics*, dating from the late nineteenth century, mainly synchronic, descriptive and concerned with system-cum-structure, linked with the 'human' sciences of sociology and psychology on the one hand, and traditional logic, philosophy and mathematics on the other – and recently beginning not only to achieve increasing

harmony within its own schools but to coalesce with (2) and to re-examine its relationships with (1).

(Although these studies are by and large part of the Western tradition, it should not be forgotten that the Greco-Roman investigation of language was paralleled by an equally sophisticated Sanskrit tradition in ancient India, and that aspects of this tradition have been, and continue to be, influential in terms of both philology and linguistics.)

During the twentieth century, linguistics has developed not so much as a unity but in various loosely associated and often geographically distinct schools, associated with certain individuals and nations on the continent of Europe, in the United Kingdom, and in North America. These schools, by no means always in tune with each other, appear nevertheless all to have arisen as a kind of reaction against both traditional grammar and philology. Some scholars, such as Henry Sweet in Britain and Otto Jespersen in Denmark, sought a harmonious extension of the older disciplines towards modern science; others, such as Ferdinand de Saussure in Switzerland and Leonard Bloomfield in the United States, more or less abandoned the philological traditions in which they had been trained, in favour of a new structuralism.

In the early twentieth century at least three significant groupings emerged in Europe: (1) a Swiss-orientated group deriving directly from Ferdinand de Saussure and including Charles Bally and Albert Sechehaye; (2) a Slavist group, centring on Prague in Czechoslovakia, and including the Pole Jan Baudouin de Courtenay, the Russians Nikolay Trubetzkoy and Roman Jakobson, the Austrian Karl Bühler, and the Czech Vilem Mathesius; and (3) a Danish school linked principally with the name of Louis Hjelmslev. These European schools have been broadly characterized by their interest in language as functional systems, and their fundamental theoretical work has played a great part in establishing linguistics as a scientific discipline.

The British school, with centres in such university cities as London, Edinburgh, Reading and Leeds, is sometimes said to have had more practical enthusiasms than the Europeans, and because of its association with Empire has shown interest in African and Asian languages as well as English and the traditionally more prominent of the European languages. From the time of Henry Sweet there has been a strong interest in both phonetics and the practicalities of research in grammar, as well as a desire to find applications of linguistics – including the development of a specific discipline of 'applied linguistics'. The names of Daniel Jones and David Abercrombie are important in phonetics, those of John Rupert Firth, Michael Halliday and John Lyons in theoretical linguistics, and S. Pit Corder and Peter Strevens in applied linguistics. Applied linguistics has tended to shade almost imperceptibly into the area where skilled language teachers have worked to improve their craft, mindful of the developments within linguistic science, and in this regard one can mention such names as Harold Palmer, Michael West and Louis G. Alexander.

Linguistics in the United States was greatly influenced by the anthropological and linguistic work among the Amerindian peoples of Franz Boas, Edward Sapir and Benjamin Lee Whorf, and for a time even more strongly influenced by the structuralism of Leonard Bloomfield and his enthusiasm for behavioural psychology. Various structuralist schools grew up before, during and after the Second World War and had a powerful influence on language teaching. These schools were characterized by an approach to language as analysable data rather than as a living process. Meaning as a subject for linguistic investigation ('semantics') was relegated to the sidelines in this approach, which was dominant until supplanted in the 1950s by the first wave of Noam Chomsky's transformational-generative grammar. Chomsky rejected much of structuralism explicitly but implicitly retained much else, turned to symbolic logic and to aspects of traditional grammar, and succeeded in reorientating a majority of American linguists towards language as a creative process with strong genetic roots, something best approached from the angle of cognitive psychology.

These are the barest outlines; an attempt to say more could lead to a book on this subject alone, just as each of the preceding sections could be expanded into a volume. Indeed, as the notes and references make clear, there are many excellent works available relating in a variety of ways to almost everything I have been discussing in this survey.

Overviews are risky things; there is always the danger of one word or sentence too many or too few or without the right nuance. No summary can do justice to such a dynamic and controversial discipline as linguistics, but it may well be able to serve as a kind of safe base from which further reading, research and discussion can be undertaken. A consensus of opinion is not by nature a clearcut thing, and one individual's interpretation of such a consensus is bound, willy nilly, to have implicit biases and preferences built into it. I have sought to avoid the more slippery slopes, and in doing so have also avoided some of the most interesting and well-publicized topics in linguistics. Thus, I have said nothing about the 'morpheme' and all its cousin -emes that can be found in profusion throughout the literature; I have avoided any discussion of grammatical transformations, of deep and surface structure, and of 'generative' approaches to language. These are too hot to handle in a survey of this nature.

Additionally, I have not attempted here to 'teach' any of the more or less agreed technical aspects of the subject, nor to describe in any detail certain established ways of looking at historical developments in language study. Thus, I have not set out to describe articulatory phonetics or the rhythm and prosody of languages, nor have I organized myself so as to discuss 'traditional grammar', 'structuralism', 'transformationalism' and so on. Other comprehensive works do these things very well, and should be consulted as necessary. The notes and references provided at the end of this book offer one avenue via which such works can be approached if readers are not already familiar with them.

My primary concern here has been twofold:

1 A knowledge of what linguists disagree *least* about may serve as a foundation for an informed consideration of what they disagree *most* about.

2 It is not easy for non-linguists to work their way through even the introductory studies that linguists have written for them. In a sense, therefore this survey has been an introduction to the introductions.

Part 2 Twenty-five centuries of grammar: an examination of our cultural conditioning

A historical and social review of how we acquired and how we respond to the concept 'grammar', along with a consideration of both the debt that we owe to our predecessors and the need to be wary of the patterns of expectation that our heritage has imposed upon us.

For all grammarians draw freely on the work of their predecessors and at the same time use their new vantage point to see where fresh headway can be made.
(Randolph Quirk and Sidney Greenbaum, preface to *A University Grammar of English*, 1973)

2.0 Introduction

'Grammar' is difficult. It is not a precise term in the way that words like 'phonology' or 'anatomy' or 'sodium chloride' may be considered precise terms.

In this respect, however, it behaves pretty much like the majority of words in a language: it has a core of generally agreed meaning, but is fuzzy at the edges. Strict scientific terms like 'phonology' and 'anatomy' are coined in order to escape from such everyday ambiguity. That they often fail to do so, acquiring in course of time their own fuzzy edges too, suggests that a tendency towards imprecision is basic to language.

'Grammar' is a word of great antiquity, with a whole constellation of senses and applications acquired in its journey down the years and across great distances. This kind of multiple meaning (or, technically, 'polysemy') can be demonstrated by looking at another word first, as an example. Consider these sentences:

1 The woman shouted that the house was on fire.
2 The captain ordered his men to fire.
3 'Fire!'

Sentences 1 and 2 provide enough linguistic context to show what is meant by the item 'fire' in each case. Sentence 3, however, presents a problem, because we have no means of knowing whether it relates to the warning shouted by the woman or the order shouted by the captain. In isolation, this word–cum–sentence is *either* uninterpretable *or* variously interpretable, and therefore conveys no practical information. The only possible response to such a sentence in isolation is something like: 'What do you mean, fire?'

Similarly with 'grammar'. Someone using the term may have a reasonably clear idea of what he or she intends by it, even using plenty of linguistic context along with it, but this is in itself no guarantee that the listener or reader shares that clarity. Consider these sentences:

1 Grammar is the rules people use when speaking or writing a language.
2 He bought a new French grammar.
3 She corrected his bad grammar.
4 The wizard was busy with grammar and other strange doings.
5 The boys went to a local grammar school.
6 That language was never written down, so it doesn't really have a grammar.
7 English is a language that doesn't have much grammar.
8 'Grammar' and 'syntax' are really the same thing.
9 People who know a language work from grammars inside their heads.
10 The grammar of a language includes how to spell it and pronounce it.
11 Descriptive grammar is very different from prescriptive grammar.
12 Traditional grammar and modern theories like transformational-generative grammar both seek to describe and explain natural language.

These twelve sentences may not exhaust all the shades of possible meaning, but they should serve to illustrate the multiplicity of uses that the word has in English alone – and maybe caution language professionals against too unconsidered a use of so flexible a term.

In addition to the inherent imprecision of language, our problem is compounded by the normally unreflective way in which people discuss language. All users of English will insist – and rightly – that they know the meaning of the word 'fire', and since it almost always occurs in some kind of context they will seldom have trouble with it. Similarly, people who have been to a school influenced by European language traditions will insist that they know what 'grammar' is, and will use something like sentence 1 above to make their point clear. As a general rule-of-thumb sentence 1 is fine, unarguably so. But in the specific milieu of linguistics we see that this definition has only shifted the problem: what, then, are these 'rules we use when speaking or writing a language'? What base do they rest on?

The question is an ancient one, at least two thousand five hundred years ancient. Attempts to answer it long ago produced a terminology (with its attendant theory) that is now part of the bricks and mortar of the culture of the Western world, so much so that we take it for granted and treat it as part of the background to what we are and what we do, as if it were like gravity or the spectrum of colours or the days of the week – unquestioned and maybe unquestionable. The Jesuit scholar Francis P. Dinneen, however, argues that we could be making a considerable mistake by doing this:

> The terminology of traditional grammar, inherited from the
> Greeks, comprises the most widespread, best understood, and
> most generally applied grammatical distinctions in the world.
> However, many teachers of school grammar today – and many
> linguists – do not have an adequate understanding of the
> background of this terminology. To communicate with others
> about language or anything else we require shared experience.
> And in order to judge which of two ways of talking about
> language is superior in view of a stated goal, we must
> understand the presuppositions of each.
> (*An Introduction to General Linguistics*, 1967, p. 71)

Dinneen's argument is part of a larger argument: that one cannot hope to understand the present without a knowledge of the past. Certainly, to reject the past or to be unwilling to examine it is as extreme a position as excessive veneration for ancient institutions simply because they are ancient. Each standpoint suggests a lack of balance.

Nowadays, by and large, there is an imbalance in our attitudes towards such things as 'grammar'. The subject is not generally popular, despite – or perhaps because of – the great efforts that have been made towards universal education. Loosely, one can identify five common reactions to the idea of studying grammar:

1 Many people who studied grammar at school found it unpleasant; similarly, they may have found mathematics unpleasant too. Today, they are often convinced that this was because the teaching methods used were totally wrong-headed.
2 Many other people are too young to have studied grammar formally, in the old way, because it was out of fashion when they were at school, except possibly in the teaching of a foreign language. They heard, however, from parents and older friends that it was unpleasant, and mostly regard it as either an imposition or an irrelevance or both.
3 For whatever reason, some people lack a clear idea of what grammar is or does, and feel anxious about it, because some others still insist on its importance. Their feelings of insecurity create a certain hostility towards the subject.
4 Some people link grammar with criticisms that others have made of their way of using a language. A sense of resentment has built up against both the critics and the subject whose rules the critics have invoked.
5 Whatever it is, the study of grammar appears to need a sustained effort, and for a variety of reasons a person is not interested in making such an effort.

Despite such reasons as these, however, and the distaste for grammar that accompanies them, a counter-current can be discerned – a renewed interest in grammar that could even (rather daringly) be called the start of a renaissance. Recent linguistic debates about 'theories of grammar' have certainly begun to influence academic and educational trendsetters; social discontent about school standards in reading, writing and other language skills has also led many people to reconsider their attitudes to 'grammar', because it carries with it certain ideas of discipline and solidity in learning.

All of this is clearly an imbalance; it could even be a useful one, in the sense that out of disagreement and disillusion might come something fresh and useful. The present survey is presented as a contribution towards clarifying some of the issues – and with a considerable sympathy for Dinneen's argument. Language teachers (at the very least) cannot afford to dodge the deceptively simple question: what is 'grammar'?

2.1   The ancient world

Like so many other things, grammar is an invention of the ancient Greeks. The term itself comes from their word 'grámma', a letter of the alphabet, and it was closely linked with both the craft of writing and the study of logic.

It is hard for people in today's technological civilization – a civilization which depends so much on printed instructions, typed records, computer printouts, and so on – to imagine a society without a written language. Yet for untold thousands of years communication was purely oral, and for keeping records people had only their memories.

It is also difficult to appreciate the sensational side to the early writing systems of communities like Egypt and Babylon, and the superstitious awe that unlettered people felt for those who could tease spoken meaning out of pictures and sundry other marks on various surfaces. That long-gone breakthrough can be fairly compared to the invention of the computer today, a device which is also popularly viewed with a mixture of awe, suspicion and incomprehension.

The ancient Egyptians and Babylonians have left us no clear indications of their attitudes to language. They probably had a variety of ideas about how language worked or could be described and taught, but such ideas are lost to us. It is only after the Greeks acquired their alphabet from the Phoenicians that we see developing a flood of practical and theoretical interest in language. It is as if, having found this secondary medium with its relative permanency, they became aware for the very first time that language could be described and discussed at all. Previously, it had been no more than an unconsidered vehicle for other things.

The early works of the Greeks, such as the Homeric epics, are generally described as part of their 'literature', but this is a term created after the event. Like the ancient Hindus, the Greeks had vast and complex oral heritages that might more accurately be called their '*orature*', since the other term implies letters and literacy. The oral tradition lasted for an unknown number of centuries, in which people were trained to remember and recite enormous quantities of rhythmic material with pinpoint accuracy – or, where improvisation occurred, to improvise in an organized way. Poetic rhythm may have served as much as a mnemonic aid to the nervous system as a device to make the material attractive. Certainly, poetry has steadily declined in importance – regardless of its social prestige – as other means have been found to record the various kinds of information important to a culture. We would not write a mathematical treatise today in poetic form, but some 1,500 years ago the Hindu sage Aryabhaṭa wrote abstrusely about mathematics in Sanskrit verse, and there was nothing unusual about this. It was an earlier norm for speech carried over into writing, and he used it efficiently to discuss algebra, trigonometry and the proper value of π.

The Greeks developed their practical interest in grammar while learning to commit Homeric and other material to paper. This transfer from transient sound-waves to more permanent surfaces was an important craft; it was necessary to organize it so that it could be handed on successfully from generation to generation, and this is essentially why grammar has always been more linked with the written than the spoken word. At the same time, many of the men who were interested in such matters were also speculating about the nature of life and reality, and they did not see their various interests as mutually exclusive. Such things as grammar, philosophy, logic, rhetoric and literature (as we so easily categorize them now) all ran into each other. It took time for distinct concepts to emerge, as these pioneers struggled to create theories and terminologies without much in the way of precedents to help them.

Their efforts cannot be measured by twentieth-century yardsticks which enticingly allow us to make judgements in our own favour. Plato, Aristotle and their successors often took their theories from the abyss, to build the intellectual foundation on which we still stand today.

2.2 Grammar and sorcery

For many centuries, the study of grammar was popularly equated with magic and occult learning, and grammar books were widely considered to be works on sorcery.

In those early days, someone who mastered a craft of any kind or performed anything with great skill was conceived as being under the influence of divinities such as the Muses, the goddesses of culture. Their very 'enthusiasm' was – literally – a god possessing them, and at the very least such a person was a *sophistés*, a 'wise one'. Pythagoras (sixth century BC) saw himself more humbly as a 'lover of wisdom' rather than one possessing it or being possessed by it, and called himself in consequence a *philósophos*, a term which became popular among what were in effect the scientists of the time.

'Scientists' have never been far in the popular mind from 'magicians', a word that derives from the Magi, the philosophers of ancient Persia; the English words 'witch' and 'wizard', regardless of their occult overtones, originally meant much the same as *sophistés*: a wise or skilled person.

Writing was awe-inspiring, but so also were measuring the ground ('geometry'), studying the stars ('astrology' and 'astronomy'), mixing substances ('alchemy' and 'chemistry'), and so on, all of which activities were united by the fact that they had to be recorded in books. The priesthoods of ancient nations such as Egypt were involved in such mysteries, and it is not at all surprising, therefore, that uneducated people were generally superstitious about learning of any kind, and very superstitious indeed about 'book learning'.

The Greek word for an alphabetic letter was *grámma*, and the skill of cutting or writing such *grámmata* on a surface was a *tékhnē* (from which 'technique' and 'technology' are derived). The whole process was *hē grammátikē tékhnē*, 'the craft of lettering', which the Romans in due course translated as *ars grammatica*.

In medieval French the *ars* ('art') was dropped and the adjective mutated into the noun *gramaire* (modern *grammaire*, with the other 'm' reinserted), from which the English form derives. The Middle Ages were a time of superstition in which the virtuous Roman poet Virgil was transformed into a powerful magician, so it is not surprising that grammar became magical too. In Middle English a *gramarye* was a sorcerer's book, and in modern French a *grimoire* still is.

This appears to be a common pattern of response in societies divided into learned minorities and unlettered majorities. Traditionally, in India, for example, the term *yoga* has meant, for the learned, a disciplined philosophy of life leading towards release from the pains and impositions of the world. In popular terms, however, throughout the northern Indian languages, *yoga* or *joga* is magical tricks (of the bed-of-nails variety), and a *yogi* or *jogi* is a magician. Similarly, in the West until relatively recently, the science of chemistry has had a suspect general reputation:

The term *chemistry* ('the art or practice of the chemist') is of
seventeenth-century English origin. Its ending, like that of
sophistry and palmistry, probably implied contempt. In 1652
chemistry was described as 'a kinde of praestigious, covetous,

cheating magick'; and, in view of the history of the word itself,
it is not surprising if the subject has not yet attained total
respectability.

(Hazel Rossotti, *Introducing Chemistry*, 1975, p. 9)

The above observations have not been made in an attempt to brighten
up an otherwise dull subject. It is a fact of modern life that many people
consider grammar dull; it was a fact of medieval life that many people
considered it perilous and magical, a common response to the intellectual
activities of certain minorities. Mass opinion as well as minority effort contribute to the constellated meanings of words, and in a fair examination
of the subject these non-academic aspects should also be identified
clearly, without however seeking to over-romanticize the history of a word
or point to the foolishness of peasants.

That the mysterious art of grammar had its beguiling side for the less
educated mind is witnessed by one more transformation imposed upon it,
this time in Scotland, where it became 'glamour'. This variation, popularized
by the Romantic novelist Walter Scott in the early nineteenth century, is
explained by Webster's *Third New International Dictionary* (1966, p. 962)
as arising 'from the popular association of erudition with occult practices'.
Webster then provides two main definitions (quoted here in part): 'a magic
spell; an elusive mysteriously exciting and often illusory attractiveness that
stirs the imagination and appeals to a taste for the unconventional, the
unexpected, the colorful or the exotic, *etc.*'

Whether it is in the organized rhythmic chanting of language, or the
committing of such chants to special surfaces, whether it is in the conflation
of the philosophical investigator with the sorcerer, humanity provides
plenty of evidence that it has linked language with magic, 'grammar' with
'glamour'. A humble but convincing last witness to this is the English word
'spell' (used in Webster's first definition above). This small but potent word
retains like a fossil the traces of our schizophrenia: as a noun it is magical,
while as a verb it refers to saying letters out loud.

2.3 Two views of reality

*The Greeks and Romans concluded, among other things, that language is
dominated by two opposing principles: 'analogy' and 'anomaly'. From this
dualism have developed the traditional concepts of 'regularity' and
'irregularity' in language.*

In the fifth century BC, the central argument in the philosophical study of
language was between *phýsis* ('nature') and *nómos* ('convention'). The
naturalists claimed that all language was – or at least originally had been – a

reflection of natural reality, in the way that onomatopoeic expressions like 'bang', 'splash' and 'zoom' are said to echo natural sounds. The conventionalists, on the other hand, argued that language was a social artifact and contract, its elements bearing no direct relationship with anything outside itself. The supporters of convention won the day, but the argument cast a long shadow: there are still 'naturalists' today, who consider that in some serious way their own particular language properly reflects nature, and that, if God were to speak, He would speak in that language.

Small children are essentially 'naturalists'. When they have learned one particular expression in relation to something observable in the world, they object strongly to being given alternatives or to contradiction. In addition, unless they are exposed early to other language systems than their own, they will consider that a foreign equivalent is not the 'real' word for a thing. Even minor changes are resented, as this apocryphal story from my home town of Glasgow in Scotland suggests:

TEACHER (pointing to an animal in a picture): Jimmy, what's this?
JIMMY (without hesitation): It's a dug, Miss.   [dʌg]
TEACHER (firmly, insisting on Standard English): No, it is not. It's a *dog*.
JIMMY: That's funny. It looks like a dug.

The dispute over nature or convention was succeeded by an equally fierce debate about whether or not language is an orderly phenomenon, part of a larger argument about whether reality itself is a matter of order or chaos. This debate centred upon two important terms: *analogía* and *anōmalía*.

The first of these, *analogía*, was essentially a mathematical term, meaning 'ratio', 'proportion' or some kind of parallelism in the sense that certain elements are shared by certain otherwise different pairs of things. The following is an *analogía*:

2:6::3:9

The same relationship holds (for certain purposes) between 2 and 6 as holds between 3 and 9. This is a strictly mathematical ratio, but such an *analogía* is also applicable to language:

cat:cats::dog:dogs

Nowadays, the particular relationship shown in this way would be called 'regular singulars and plurals in English'. The ratio shows how a second plural is formed 'by analogy', the primary pair serving as a model or example. This kind of relationship is not normally now shown by means of ratios; it is in fact pretty well taken for granted, but its origin lies in this quasi-mathematical procedure developed long ago.

The analogists argued that if such ratios could be set up so easily for language, it was because they already existed in language, waiting to be discovered. Human language, they asserted, was acquired, used and extended – and could therefore be described and even *taught* – by means of comparisons: 'The plural of *dog* is formed like the plural of *cat*, like the plural of *duck, ship, house*...'

Anōmalía, however, means 'unevenness' or 'the state of not being the same', and the anomalists argued that the analogists were, in effect, seeing things that were not really there. They asserted that the elements in language were essentially *dis*similar, that the exceptions always outnumbered the congruencies. In other words, there might well be a concept of plurality, but the forms through which it was expressed were more likely to go as follows (if handled analogically):

cat:cats::deer:deer
        goose:geese
        mouse:mice
        man:men

Both groups had clearly got hold of something important, but each claimed that its own position was the fundamental truth about language. The argument, however, was more than linguistic; it was political too. When the empire of Alexander the Great broke up in the fourth century BC, pride of place in the Hellenic world was disputed by two cities, neither of which was in Greece proper. One was Pergamon, in Asia Minor, and the other was Alexandria, in Egypt. Anomalism was the view favoured in Pergamon, while the Alexandrians supported analogism as the proper explanation not only of language but of how the *kósmos* (that is, 'the well-ordered place', the world or universe) was created and sustained. The Alexandrians won both politically and linguistically, but the anomalists of Pergamon have also cast a long shadow: there are still people today who deny essential regularity in languages, claiming rather that grammarians seek to impose a spurious regularity upon them.

Such claims are interesting; certainly, the ancient analogists were tempted to make Greek more properly regular, by adjusting those forms that did not fit the majority patterns, while the Stoics argued that things failed to fit because languages degenerated through time from earlier true forms (their *étyma*). In principle, irregularities can easily be analogized into line with majority patterns, much as follows:

cat:cats::dog:dogs
        deer:deers
        goose:gooses
        mouse:mouses
        man:mans

To play this game is to learn – vividly and directly – some interesting things about human beings and languages. Children, for example, *do* quite clearly analogize, and their doing so is only really noticed when they engage in what is called – rather unkindly – a 'false analogy'. Foreign learners of a language also play the analogy game, and nothing irritates them more than to discover that a perfectly good bit of analogical reasoning and creativity just didn't work this time. The game can also be played, instructively, in reverse, with such 'false analogies' as:

ox: oxen :: box: boxen
   cat: caten
   dog: dogen
   house: housen
   etc.

mouse: mice :: louse: lice
   house: hice
   spouse: spice
   douse: dice
   blouse: blice
   etc.

These are amusing in their way, but the 'wrongly' formed plurals are only odd and amusing because we have never met them before. In themselves they are – linguistically, analogically – just as good as the ones that *do* exist, though psychologically and socially they seem bizarre. They may in fact point to ancient or regionally limited analogies that either no longer function or are not present in the standard language. A real-life example can be taken from Scots, the Germanic language of Scotland, so close to English that it is often regarded – and very defensibly – as simply a northern dialect. In Scots, the regular simple past forms of two common verbs can be shown as:

tell: telt :: sell: selt

This fits closely with the dominant way of forming past tenses in both Scots and English, but in Standard English both verbs are irregular:

tell: told :: sell: sold

In consequence, the Scots forms sound curious to ears accustomed only to Standard English, and many Scots have long since amended their usage away from the regular in Scots towards the irregular in Standard English in order to conform to its norms. This indicates not only the power of certain analogies, but also the power of certain well-established anomalies. (Of course, in effect, many anomalies are simply minor analogies that lack sufficient universality.)

Similarly, American usage can be contrasted with British as regards the verb *dive*, as follows:

AMERICAN   strive:strove::dive:dove
BRITISH   strive:strove::dive:*dived*

Americans are used to, and often use, the form *dived*, but the British have not used the older form *dove* for a very long time, and to their ears it seems quaint.

Two leading grammarians of the ancient world – Dionysius Thrax of Alexandria and the Roman Marcus Terentius Varro, contemporaries around 100 BC – drew the conclusion that analogy was fundamental both to language *per se* and to its description, but that anomalies also had to be properly presented. Varro in particular made it clear, as he adapted Greek grammar to fit Latin, that there was no universal regularity and certainly no universal chaos. His moderate position represents, by and large, the base upon which future Western grammatical descriptions have been raised.

2.4   The invention of grammar

The idea of 'parts of speech' also derives from ancient Greek studies, but it was many centuries before the classification generally used today took shape, and it is still by no means universally agreed.

There is good reason to suppose that if writing had not been invented then grammar would not have been invented either. Divisions of language are more easily established on paper than in sound, but even on paper the kind of clarity that we take for granted today only emerged slowly. For example, it was the ancient Greek custom simply to write letters continuously, without spaces separating words, and this made their writing much like all speech everywhere – a continuous flow, when conducted naturally. In speech there is no necessary space between 'words', 'phrases' and 'sentences', unless we deliberately choose to pause. Nonetheless, this potential pause is an important factor in establishing the separateness of linguistic units, and for many centuries now it has been, on paper, an actual pause, re-expressed as a space.

For many of us, the idea of a 'word' is intimately linked with writing and the spaces that demarcate one word from another. Such devices help establish the psychological reality of 'words', including the recognition of functional variations among groups or classes of words, variations that we now call 'nouns', 'verbs', and so on. Such categories were not, however, instantly self-evident; they had to be established by observation and theorizing, and this took centuries. For many people the business of identifying parts of speech in texts is as difficult as algebra; the relationships and functions are not apparent to them, even after careful explanation. How much more difficult, therefore, was the original classification?

Plato (c. 428–348 BC) and Aristotle (384–322 BC) diverged on many points, but they appear to have agreed on three fundamental terms necessary for the description of language. These are:

1 the *ónoma* or 'name', translated into Latin as the *nomen*, and (as examples of present-day usage) into French as *le nom* and into English as *the noun*. Its plural is *onómata*.

2 the *rhēma*, translatable as 'what is spoken', 'word', 'saying', 'phrase', 'predicate' and a number of other concepts. It was differentiated from the *ónoma* by its having a time reference (that is, 'times' or 'tenses'). The Romans called it the *verbum*, which was also their word for 'word', the French call it *le verbe* and in English it is *the verb*. Its plural is *rhēmata*.

3 the *lógos*, one of the most important terms in Greek thought generally, translatable as a whole spectrum of modern concepts, including 'word', 'speech', 'statement', 'reason', 'report', 'narrative' and, in plural form, 'prose'. For the grammarian–logicians of the ancient world, however, it was a composite made up of *onómata*, *rhēmata*, and *sýndesmoi*, a general class of particles roughly corresponding to 'conjunctions'. It was translated into Latin as the *oratio*, and is part-ancestor of what is today called *a sentence* in English and *une phrase* in French.

The *lógos* worked hard in ancient times. In its philosophical aspect it lies at the root of the whole science of 'logic', as well as the innumerable modern '-ologies' ('biology', 'geology', etc.). It is present in 'analogy' and 'syllogism', in 'prologue' and 'epilogue' and 'catalogue', in 'monologue' and 'dialogue', in 'eulogy', 'logistics', 'logarithm', and many others. In its religious aspect it became fused with the Hebrew concept of the Messiah, expressing the idea of a rational, compassionate power in the cosmos: the Logos. The Christian Gospel of St John was written in Greek, and in it the term *lógos* is the original of 'the Word' (in French 'La Parole' or 'Le Verbe') in these famous translations:

In the beginning was the Word, and the Word was with God,
and the Word was God.

Au commencement était la Parole, et la Parole était avec Dieu, et
La Parole était Dieu.

The idea of the Word made Flesh (in Latin, *Verbum caro factum est*) has been part of Christian doctrine ever since, the Logos having been equated with Christ. Again, this is not simply a colourful etymological aside. It serves to indicate the potency of the terms which the Greeks were struggling with, and how these terms have in a whole constellation of ways become woven into the very fabric of our civilization, often without us any longer being directly aware of the connections.

The idea of sentence types as we understand them today (as declarations, questions, commands, and the like) developed slowly. An early classification was in terms of logical propositions (*lógoi*), but these were less immediately useful in grammar than a stylistic device that evolved in rhetoric and prose writing. This was the *períodos*, that other part-ancestor of today's 'sentence', an attempt to encapsulate a complete thought, assertion or piece of narrative with all its main and dependent ideas into one controlled flow of words written between the two points that are nowadays called 'periods' (or full-stops). Ancient rhetoricians such as Isocrates (fourth century BC) made much of the idea of a 'well-rounded expression' (the approximate meaning of the term *períodos*). Writers like the Roman historian Livy and generations of classical teachers of prose-writing established this style very securely, passing it on to the Middle Ages and writers in the new vernaculars of Europe. 'The period' or 'periodic sentence' attained its peak among these languages in the eighteenth century, and also served as a model for sentence analysis into various kinds of clauses, so that when taken together with the propositions of logic it provided a practical framework for the classification of 'sentences' into 'simple', 'complex', 'compound' and 'compound-complex'.

So, slowly, the edifice of grammatical description was built up. Dionysius Thrax, in his *Art of Grammar*, crystallized a wide range of theories and practices into a compact form, defining grammar as 'the technical knowledge of the language generally used by poets and writers', and the sentence as 'a combination of words, either in prose or verse, making complete sense'. These two definitions make it very clear indeed where the enthusiasms of grammarians traditionally lie: with writing. Dionysius Thrax cared to some extent about the spoken language, but the following list of the six parts to his *Grammar* shows his preferences and represents the essential shape of things as they would be over the next 2,000 years:

1 correct pronunciation
2 figures of speech in poetry
3 difficult texts
4 etymology
5 grammatical rules (analogies)
6 a critical consideration of the works of the great poets

He also laid down the essential list of parts of speech, greatly developed in the intervening 250 years or so since Plato and Aristotle, but remarkably like today's: noun, verb, participle, article, pronoun, preposition, adverb and conjunction. The participle has been demoted since, and in the Middle Ages the adjective was added after a re-examination of the kinds of noun in Latin, but otherwise – apart from such peripheral items as interjections – very little has changed. Since the nineteenth century various liberal grammarians such as Otto Jespersen have sought to add new distinctions, but with little popular success. Modern linguists have attempted a whole population explosion of new terms relating to distinct theories and schools of thought, with varying popular success outside their own discipline. The 'determiner' seems to have established itself, and 'intensifiers' and 'quantifiers' may get there, but even if they do, it will not be at the expense of the established terms. Thrax laid his foundation well. No one seriously disputes his choice.

2.5 From Greece to Rome

The Greek and Roman grammarians were describing two very similar languages, classical Greek and Latin. Since their day, grammarians have used their ideas and terms for the description of other languages, some similar to Greek and Latin, some very different.

Dionysius Thrax was not describing language as a universal phenomenon; he was describing the Greek that he knew, and nothing else. Roman grammarians such as Terentius Varro were adapters of Greek grammar into Latin, no more and no less. This was not a difficult matter, because the two languages are very similar, but the historical reasons for these similarities were not apparent to either the Greeks or Romans (at least, not to any significant degree). It was reasonable enough for them to conclude that the applicability of Greek grammar to Latin was because of its universal validity, rather than simply the historical accident that the two languages were so alike. It took a very long time indeed before students of language became aware that these two highly inflected tongues were *not* in fact models for all languages everywhere. As Dinneen points out:

We can say that the *Grammar* of Dionysius Thrax has had an influence in inverse proportion to its brevity and clarity. The questions he raised and the order in which he treated them have been little improved upon for more than twenty centuries. As we shall see, it is not unfair to say that many traditional grammarians...are still, to a large extent, translating languages into Greek, even though they may know no Greek.
(*An Introduction to General Linguistics*, 1967, p. 105)

Thrax and Varro were followed by such outstanding figures as Dyscolus (second century AD), Donatus (fourth), Boethius (fifth) and Priscian (sixth), who all regarded themselves as simply adding their mites to an established heritage. To analyse their contributions as well as the general nature of Greco-Latin grammar would require a great deal of space as well as a knowledge in the reader of Greek and Latin. Such a knowledge is no longer common, and this in fact marks off the educated person in the twentieth century from educated people in almost all the centuries between ourselves and those now near-forgotten names. So great, however, was the influence of the ancient world and of such language specialists as these, that a truly civilized person was one who, among other things, knew at least Latin and preferably something of Greek. There are still elderly people alive today who grew up in a world that nurtured such a belief, but it is one that has been largely swept away in the upheavals of our time.

This does not mean, however, that the *influence* of Greek and Latin has also been swept away, because that influence is present in all sorts of implicit ways in our culture. Linguists such as Leonard Bloomfield, for example, have tried to break away completely from traditional grammar, seeking to establish a new and 'scientific' structuralism that would replace it. By and large they failed, although in the attempt they did a great deal to show what language description is and is not. Today, linguistics is less at odds with traditionalism, seeking rather to adapt and build on these older foundations, but the insidious question keeps quietly repeating itself: does the relative failure of a departure like Bloomfield's mean, as Dinneen suggests, that we are still trapped inside the minds of the ancient Greeks and Romans?

2.6   The paradigm

One legacy from classical scholarship is the 'paradigm', a table demonstrating how such things as verbs, nouns and adjectives should be used. Such paradigms deal in both regularities and irregularities in a variety of languages, providing models that students can learn 'by heart'.

Greek and Latin were inflected languages; that is, their nouns, verbs and adjectives fitted into the flow of discourse by the mediation of affixes of various kinds, marking such things as 'subject of the sentence', 'object of the sentence', 'possessor', and so on. This description is, of course, given in modern terms; it took the Greeks a long time to find a means of describing this aspect of their language, but the method they finally hit on has permanently marked language description (and language teaching and learning) to this day.

They hit upon an odd metaphor to describe what they found. Beginning with the *ónoma* or noun, they imagined a basic upright category, the 'name' as such, and then described all the other inflectional forms as 'falling' away from it, as in the diagram overleaf, where each line represents a *ptōsis* or 'fall'.

It can be seen from this diagram that the Greek *ónoma* ('noun') had five *ptōseis* ('falls'), each with its clearly defined function. When the time came, however, to transfer the description into Latin, it was discovered that

51

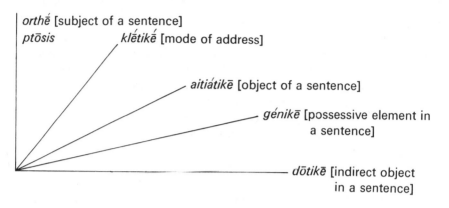

the fit was not exact. A sixth *ptōsis* had to be added, and this, incidentally, weakens the argument of those who say that classical grammar was quite inflexible. It was not; otherwise, Latin would have been made to fit, inaccurately, into five categories, not six. The diagram is repeated below, with the sixth category, and each of the Greek *ptōseis* given its Latin name:

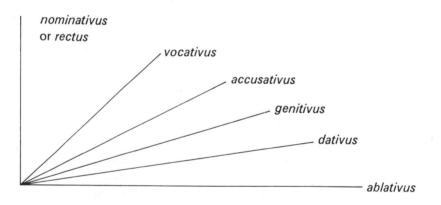

The falling metaphor was translated too, *ptōsis* becoming *casus* (also 'a fall'), which in modern English is 'a case'. The first five cases of Latin have the same roles as the Greek, but the 'ablative' is more difficult to explain: it is both agentive and separative, and is normally explained by means of the English prepositions 'by, with, from', or their equivalents in other languages.

Generations of Latin learners have been more familiar with these cases in box or tabular form, exemplifying the five 'declensions' of Latin nouns. This term – *declinatio* in the original – also sustains the falling metaphor, meaning something like 'bending aside' or 'leaning over'. Comparable tables for verbs are their 'conjugations' – *coniugationes*, 'things yoked or joined together'. Thus, Thrax and Varro set the stage for innumerable classes in unnumbered schools across the world where youngsters have declined their nouns and conjugated their verbs in a variety of languages.

It might be as well at this point to display a noun paradigm in full, so that its complexities and its precision can be considered. The two tables that follow are for model nouns of the first and second declensions in Latin, first declension nouns being typically feminine, while second declension nouns, as represented here, are typically masculine. They are presented with appropriate English paraphrases:

	Case	*Singular*		*Plural*	
I	nominative	*mensa*	('a table')	*mensae*	('tables')
	vocative	*mensa*	('O table!')	*mensae*	('O tables!')
	accusative	*mensam*	('a table')	*mensas*	('tables')
	genitive	*mensae*	('of a table')	*mensarum*	('of tables')
	dative	*mensae*	('to/for a table')	*mensīs*	('to/for tables')
	ablative	*mensā*	('by/with/ from a table')	*mensīs*	(by/with/ from tables')
II	nominative	*dominus*	('a master')	*domini*	('masters')
	vocative	*domine*	('O master!')	*domini*	('O masters!')
	accusative	*dominum*	('master')	*dominos*	('masters')
	genitive	*domini*	('of a master; master's')	*dominorum*	('of masters; masters'')
	dative	*dominō*	('to/ for a master')	*dominīs*	('to/for masters')
	ablative	*dominō*	('by/with/from a master')	*dominīs*	('by/with/ from masters')

Someone whose home language is uninflected or much less inflected than Latin will find this kind of material hard to assimilate at first. The lean, stripped-down way in which the material is presented also needs support from plenty of examples of usage. Classical grammarians usually invented examples to fit what they were teaching, creating thereby a basic grading and selecting procedure and also, often, producing phrases and sentences that were grammatically excellent but unlikely to occur in everyday life. (I recall being fascinated at secondary school by Latin sentences that translated as, for example, 'The sailors gave roses to the queen', trying to imagine this happy breed of mariner.)

The model sentences that accompanied the paradigms (which, in turn, mean in Greek 'models' or 'examples') were much as follows:

1 *Dominus mensam vidit.*
   (Master – table – saw he.)
   = The master saw the table.   (Articles added in English, there being none in Latin.)

2 *Mensam domini mei vidi.*
  (Table – of master mine – saw I.)
  = I saw my master's table.
3 *Mensa dominō data est.*
  (Table – to master – given is.)
  = The table is given to the master.

Even this small fragment of Latin – compared and contrasted with English – contains a great deal of information. We can learn from the table and examples that, for example:

1 Latin cases are paralleled in English by special sentence-positions and prepositional phrases (not forgetting, however, that prepositions also occur in Latin, but that each preposition governs an appropriate case; thus *in villam*, using the accusative, means 'into the villa', while *in villā*, using the ablative, mean 'in the villa').

2 Latin grammar seriously differs from English grammar. Latin has no article, but English has, and Greek too. This is another indication that the ancients were not inflexible; they were perfectly capable of recognizing differences among languages, and adjusting accordingly. The Greek article (equivalent to the English definite article) declined according to the case of its nouns and also according to three genders: masculine, feminine and neuter. It therefore had resemblances to the definite and indefinite articles in modern German. Where Greek and Latin had three genders, modern French and Spanish, for example, have only two, and English has none. Traditional grammar has been able to handle these differences without difficulty, and Dinneen's observation that Greek still dominates traditional models of grammar cannot therefore be seen as an absolute statement.

3 The Latin verb typically comes at the end of a sentence, while the English verb typically comes in the middle.

4 You can, in principle, address both masters and tables in Latin by means of a special vocative case, whether or not you would want to. (The idea of saying 'Come, O table!' must have puzzled or diverted many a learner of Latin.)

5 Pronouns certainly exist in Latin, but they are not normally used as the subjects of verbs, since verb endings do the same work. Personal pronouns in the nominative case are therefore kept for purposes of emphasis and contrast, which is also true of modern Spanish and Italian, but not true of modern French and English.

And so on. It will be noticed that the paradigms and model sentences provide an easy means of making comparative and contrastive statements about language, statements that might be hard to make without such a means. By making such comparisons and contrasts students quickly realize the richness and diversity of languages as separate systems, and down the centuries this kind of analysis encouraged flexibility in matters of both theory and practice. No one could long suppose that one language had a monopoly on truth; it could be seen that some languages were very compact and efficient in certain things, while others had virtues in other areas. Additionally, such comparisons served well where training in translation was concerned.

It is not surprising therefore, especially when medieval and later students learned Latin as a second language, that they learned it from grammatical models and via translation. This was – and remains – a very artificial way of learning a language, far removed from the way that children acquire their home languages or merchants pick up foreign tongues in the marketplace, but 'artificial' does not *ipso facto* mean 'bad'. It is in fact much less hit-or-miss than the marketplace, and many generally approved things are artificial, such as writing itself, electricity (as artificial light) and margarine (as a kind of artificial butter). What we are talking about here, of course, is the much-maligned 'grammar–translation method' of studying and acquiring a foreign language, a method used with a great deal of academic success for centuries before it began to be criticized in the era of more universal education. When criticizing it, however, we need to be very careful just what it is that we are objecting to.

2.7 The European vernaculars and their classical heritage

In recent times, there has been a reaction against Latin, classical views of grammar, and the 'grammar–translation method' of teaching and learning languages. This reaction suggests that over the centuries this whole tradition has done more harm than good in language education generally, and it is necessary to consider carefully whether this belief is justified or not.

We have seen that, although they were very similar, classical Greek and Latin were not grammatically identical, and that Roman grammarians knew this when they adapted Greek techniques for Latin purposes. Later, in the Middle Ages, Latin was the prestige international language of Europe, so much so that the term 'grammar' meant for centuries only the grammar of Latin, and when in the sixteenth century and afterwards 'grammar schools' developed in countries like England these schools were devoted first and foremost to the inculcating of Latin and its grammar into the heads of their students.

The European vernacular languages that slowly established themselves from about the tenth century onward were in many ways like Homeric Greek – they had oratures, but not literatures, and seemed to men trained in the Greco-Latin tradition to be 'barbarous' tongues – even when such tongues were their own languages. They had a tendency to apologize to themselves for the deficiencies of their own forms of speech, and to doubt whether such languages could be or become true vehicles for literature, philosophy and the like. It took centuries for languages like Italian, French, Spanish, English and German to acquire credible standard written and spoken forms, all of which were judged severely by the current standards of civilization – that is, the standards at least of Latin if not also of Greek. Whatever one may nowadays think about this long-gone fact, the vernaculars finally passed the test, often, paradoxically, by opening their gates to an influx of Latin and Greek vocabulary to 'enrich' their native resources. English was latinized, and French was re-latinized, and slowly became respectable tongues in the opinions of their own citizens and foreign competitors alike. One may argue about aspects of this vast historical process, but one cannot argue it out of existence.

The phenomenon was made doubly complex by the presence in Western Europe at least of two dominant language groups: the Romance group that itself derived from forms of popular Latin, and the Germanic group that had remote historical links with Latin but was and is a very different family. Anything one says about the impact of Latin and classical grammar has to take into account the fact that its impact can hardly be the same as regards such languages as Spanish and French on the one hand and German and English on the other.

We can look, first of all, at the relationship between Latin and the Romance languages. These are still inflected languages, but in the centuries that followed the fall of the Western Roman Empire the inflection of nouns was massively weakened in such languages as Italian, Spanish and French. Singular and plural differences continued, but the nominative, vocative and accusative of Latin became one form only, while the other three cases – genitive, dative and ablative – were replaced by prepositional constructions based on that one simple form. Thus, the Latin *mensa domini mei* ('my master's table') is in French *la table de mon maître*, where *de*, a preposition, replaces the *-i* in both *domini* and *mei*.

The old descriptions often continued, so that the French sentence above might be said to contain a genitive, but this is clearly an analogical extension from Latin; there are no inflections of a genitive type in French.

The verb, however, was an easier matter to handle. It did and does not present much of a problem because much less mutation has taken place among verbs than among nouns. Conjugational tables can still serve the verbs of Italian, Spanish and French because, in a serious sense, the verbs of these languages are still very much Latin verbs. It is, in fact, difficult to find a better way of presenting them systematically.

To illustrate this point, I will first of all present – in tabular form – one tense of one Latin verb. (Technically, it is the present indicative active tense of a verb from the fourth conjugation.) The verb is *partire*, translatable into English as 'to share, distribute, divide, etc.':

Person	Singular	Plural
1st	partio	partimus
2nd	partis	partitis
3rd	partit	partiunt

(This material could actually be presented in boxes, as Latin textbooks often do. Such grids can, however, easily be dispensed with, and once the learner knows the basic relationships at work the supporting category labels can be dispensed with too.)

I will now repeat this information, in simpler form, followed by cognate structures in Italian, Spanish and French, giving their meanings to one side in English. At the end, I will put the equivalent tense structure for English, both for the sake of clarity, and to demonstate how very different English is from all of these preceding closely related languages:

Latin	partire 'to share, distribute divide, etc.'	partio partis partit	partimus partitis partiunt
Italian	partire 'to leave, depart'	parto parti parte	partiamo partite partono
Spanish	partir 'to divide, split; to leave, depart'	parto partes parte	partimos partís parten
French	partir 'to leave, depart'	je pars tu pars il / elle | part	nous partons vous partez ils / elles | partent
English	part 'to separate; to leave'	I part you part (*old*: thou partest) he / she / it | parts	we part you part they part

Although the structures and meanings of the Romance verbs are no longer quite the same, the family resemblances are strong and the underlying grid is unchanged. The alterations in meaning are, of course, interesting in themselves; there appears to have been an extension from the idea of dividing to the idea of going away similar to the use of 'split' in modern American English slang, where 'Let's split' means 'Let's leave'. Italian and Spanish retain the Latin inflections more distinctly than French, especially as regards speech, allowing the pronouns to continue in their old roles as emphasizers and a means of contrast, whereas the diminution of inflection in French (as in English) appears to have made the pronouns necessary for clear distinctions of person. What is not done one way will end up being done in another way – but it will be done.

Whereas the relevance of much of Latin description to the description of the Romance languages can be demonstrated in ways like this, it is clear that a Germanic language like English operates according to different principles. Of course, the word 'part' comes from Latin, and there are historical resemblances between Germanic and Latinate forms (because in the very remote past these language families had a common 'ancestor'), but nonetheless English is not an inflected language in the way that the Romance languages are inflected – or even to the extent that German is inflected. It is often described as an analytic ('loosening up'), isolating or open language (although its ancestral form, Anglo-Saxon, was about as inflected as Latin). In recent decades, many have argued that as a consequence the application of classical grammar to the evolving English language has been more pernicious than beneficial. Frank Palmer comments as follows:

> Latin was the classical language known by all educated people
> and was once regarded as the model for all other languages.
> Even today there are people who say that Latin is more 'logical'
> than English. In the debate a few years ago about the teaching
> of Latin at school and the requirement of Latin for entrance to
> Oxford and Cambridge, the familiar arguments were put
> forward – Latin helped to discipline the mind, Latin taught the
> students grammar. This latter statement was true in a rather
> paradoxical way. Since most English grammar teaching was
> based upon Latin the students were often at a loss. They could
> not see why English had a subjunctive or a dative case, but
> when they learnt Latin it all became clear. Latin helped them
> with their English grammar, but only because English grammar
> was really Latin grammar all the time!
> (*Grammar*, 1971, p. 15)

There are two points worth taking up here:
1 First of all, there is a difference between over-venerating the past and a reasoned appreciation of the place of Latin in European life. Too much veneration can lead to an over-enthusiastic defence of past

values, which is implicit in the view that Latin is 'more logical than English' or even the view that Latin 'has more grammar than English'. Judged from a Latin standpoint, Latin certainly conforms closer to Latin than English does.

2 Traditional grammar as such does not demand a subjunctive in English any more than it demanded an article in Latin because there was an article in Greek. It is the misuse of traditional grammar by using it without sufficient delicacy that creates the trouble that Palmer rightly objects to. But that argument is valid against the misuse of anything, whether it is grammar, alcohol, the automobile, natural resources or whatever.

There is probably more to be gained by accepting and trying to evaluate the Greco-Latin heritage than by ignoring it (and therefore avoiding teaching it to the next generation), or by seeking vehemently to replace it with something new. Attempts to do so often resemble putting the old wine back in old bottles, the only difference being new labels on the bottles.

We are our past. All the books we read are fossils in the strata of our linguistic past, and the words we use come out of a complex heritage, with their ghosts and glories, their records of part-successes and part-failures in a continuous linguistic process. New things cannot be – and are not – created *ex nihilo*, but a great deal that is useful can be done by assessing, appreciating, criticizing and developing what we have received, as part of our civilization.

As regards objections to the grammar–translation method in the teaching and learning of foreign languages, one also has to be aware of what one is objecting to. Firstly, those who used and developed classical grammar believed in it as a descriptive device, but they were well aware that a grammar with its rules and paradigms is not the language itself: it is a model, an aid towards appreciating and using that language. They were also basically concerned with reading and writing; speech was a secondary consideration for people who wanted to train scribes, clerks and scholars or readers of a revered foreign literature. Those were the primary goals, and for such goals the grammar–translation method worked adequately for centuries.

If the goals are different – as, for example, training people to speak and understand the speech of a particular living language – but classical methods are used in an attempt to achieve them, then these methods do not work because they have been misapplied – not because they are deficient in themselves. (Even in the mainly oral approach, however, a good argument can be made for supportive use of grammatical aids, especially for older learners or those who have advanced some way into a command of the target language.)

Another goal of the classical approach was and is an ability to translate and to compare structures between languages. This has been criticized as teaching people 'about' a language rather than teaching that language directly, as a self-contained system. Again, it really depends on what one wants. There can be nothing wrong in principle with wanting students to perform fluently within the system of the foreign language, without always translating – but is this any *more* useful than training people in comparative skills, when the world is full of work for translators, interpreters and the like? And finally – need these two goals be mutually exclusive?

If we consider the grammar–translation method in relation to modern languages, we should also consider it vis-à-vis the classical languages themselves. There has been a vast decrease in the numbers of students learning Latin, and those studying Greek nowadays must be nearly at vanishing point (at least if my own experience as a teacher of classics in Scotland for a few years was anything to go by). Is this decline likely to continue? It may at first glance seem 'obvious' that studying a modern language is more 'practical' than studying a 'dead' one – but on closer analysis this may not be so. Various points raised in this survey have suggested the usefulness of some knowledge at least of Latin, and it should be noted too that the teaching of the classical languages has not stood still in recent years. In the United Kingdom, for example, the Cambridge Latin Course and the work of the Scottish Classics Group show how the study of an ancient language can be brought into line with present-day interests and methods. Such efforts may, quite possibly, mark a re-awakening of interest in Latin, just as we have seen a re-awakening of interest in grammar at large.

Whether in the teaching of a modern or an ancient language, the great danger with the use of traditional paradigms (as with structuralist material too) is that the model can be mistaken for the language itself. Memorizing a table, a rule or a model does mean that a student has learned something minimally useful about the language – but not in a communicative sense. Paradigms are only way-stations towards performance, whether in the graphic or the phonic medium; they have no other function in language teaching or learning. For increased awareness in linguistics and comparative studies, of course, they are more directly useful – but that is a different matter. One should not confuse learning a language and learning how to learn a language (that is, the study and use of the aids, supports or 'crutches' offered to learners). These supports are provided only so that, in due course, they can be taken away.

Paradigms can, however, be made more humane and immediately digestible in language teaching than in the austere, monastic styles of the past. Simple, contextualized adaptations can be made. To illustrate this, I would like to quote briefly from *Les verbes: la conjugaison rendue facile* by Jacques Laurin (1971), where the traditional model verb *aimer* is presented for the present indicative active and the *passé composé*:

Présent	*Passé composé*
J'aime les fleurs.	J'ai aimé ce film.
Nous aimons la paix.	Nous avons aimé le repas d'hier.
Ils aiment le hockey.	Ils ont aimé les cours.

Times and fashions change, but the paradigm looks as though it will be with us for some time yet, and doing useful work.

2.8 Form and function

Traditionally, 'grammar' has been seen as having two components: 'morphology' and 'syntax', where morphology deals with the internal structuring of words, and syntax with the combining of words into sentences. Linguists have, however, disagreed about just where the one ends and the other begins.

The paradigms shown in the preceding section are a major legacy of Greco-Latin scholarship, but they are a legacy of a very particular kind. Such devices concentrate on form, being traditionally known as the 'accidence' of a language. This is yet another word deriving from the falling metaphor in *ptōsis, casus* and *declension/declinatio*, and means, roughly put, 'what befalls' or 'how things fall', that is, how they are arranged in terms of the theory of cases. This interest in forms is nowadays generally called 'morphology', the study of forms, which in turn is contrasted with 'syntax', which is the business of examining how words come together in strings.

Dionysius Thrax was essentially a morphologist, and, oddly enough, only the morphology has survived out of the works of Terentius Varro. The classical tradition has plenty to say about phrase and sentence structure, parsing, the analysis and synthesis of sentences and so on, but – largely because Greek and Latin were highly inflected languages – there has always been a bias towards form. The concept of the inflected word dominated over the concept of the sentence, a situation which a number of modern linguists have sought to rectify, by asserting the central place of the sentence in a syntactically orientated theory of language. An examination of a typical Latin verb form might demonstrate fairly succinctly why classical grammar placed so much emphasis on morphology. Below is such a form, with its English equivalent:

amābimus – 'we shall love' or 'we will love'

The tight unity of the Latin structure contrasts sharply with the isolative quality of the English. The parts of the English verb form can be treated separately as 'words' in a psychologically satisfying way, but the parts of the Latin verb form cannot. There is only one totality that can be called a word, and so we see, quite forcefully, that the concept 'word' has to be handled differently in English from in Latin. If we wish to find in the Latin form the equivalents of the English forms we can – more or less – do so, but only by means of pointing to elements that have distinct communicative value despite all of them being glued very tightly together:

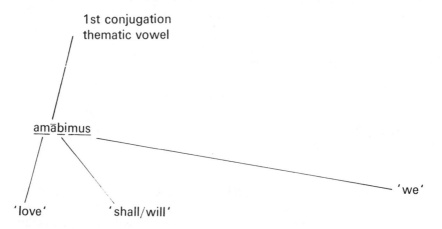

This is a fairly simple Latin word; in some, the relations among the parts are very complex and difficult to tease out. Additionally, the structural complexity can only be fully shown contrastively in relation to other similar structures, where one small difference can mark a considerable difference in meaning and function:

amābimur (passive) – 'we shall/will be loved'

It is easy to understand, therefore, why morphology was important to the classical grammarians, and also why it might be less so to grammarians who nowadays work with an apparently very different and looser structure in the English language. A universalist view of language, however, would require the grammarian to transcend both the morphological bias in Latin and the syntactic bias in English to see what lies behind both. That is, structures like *amābimur* on the one hand and 'we shall be loved' on the other hand are neither of them basic to language. Whatever language ultimately is, it lies beyond any of its individual incarnations. Latin cannot be explained by means of reference to English, nor English by means of reference to Latin, and so on. All languages are equally and variously incarnations of 'language' as a basic human capacity.

The concepts we use to handle language can be regarded as containers. Many grammarians regard 'morphology' as a container for the aspect of grammar relating to word structure, and 'syntax' as a container for everything to do with fitting words into sentences. This is a useful enough procedure, as long as we do not take it too seriously. It can be represented as follows, diagrammatically:

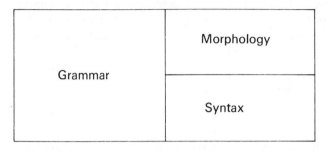

Here we have a box called 'grammar' that is divisible into or conceivable as two lesser boxes called 'morphology' and 'syntax'. The problem is: in reality, where does word structure end and sentence structure begin? This question can be illustrated in various languages, but two aspects of English will serve our purposes here:

1 The word 'tea' is a noun, and most people would also regard 'teapot' as a noun, if for no better reason than that it is written as one word. 'Teapot' is, however, structurally compatible with 'coffee pot', which is not written as one word. Why then should 'teapot' be a word and 'coffee pot' a phrase? They are, for example, both pronounced with the same kind of tone and stress pattern. If we call them 'compound words', where do we stop? Is 'teapot manufacturer' also a compound word, and if so, how do we best explain the relations governing the three constituent nouns, 'tea', 'pot' and 'manufacturer'? Should these relations, paraphrasable as 'a person who manufactures pots that are meant to hold tea', be called syntactic or morphological?

2 The word 'jump' is either a verb or a noun, depending on function, but when we deal with something like 'is jumping' are we dealing with a word or a phrase? If we refer to the verb in a sentence which contains these items, is the verb 'jump' or 'is jumping'? If we consider the whole combination a form of the verb, what do we do with things like 'should have been jumping'? Is the description of such complex verb forms syntactic or morphological?

There is no harm, of course, in fuzzy boundaries like these, as long as we have not taken our classification – our containers – too seriously. We can simply say, sensibly enough, that the line between syntax and morphology is difficult to draw, like many other lines. Many grammarians have proceeded on that basis, but it is interesting to note that the Danish scholar Otto Jespersen (1860–1943) felt able to offer a very different means of reconciling the two terms.

Jespersen was, in many ways, both classical grammarian and modern linguist, and was not highly impressed by arguments about which was more important in grammar: morphology or syntax. He proposed instead that 'form' relates to an external view of language material, while 'order' and 'meaning' are internal matters. An indissoluble and unitarian grammar could therefore be approached equally from either angle. From the outside, looking in, it is morphology, while from the inside, looking out, it is syntax. Diagrammatically:

form to meaning	*meaning to form*
outside to inside	inside to outside
O → I	I → O
morphology	syntax

Morphology is then the receiver's or observer's view of things, while syntax is the creator's position. 'The same grammatical facts may be, and have to be, viewed from both points of view, but the classification and arrangement must be totally different according as the facts are seen from without or within' (*A Modern English Grammar on Historical Principles*, preface dated 1942 but taken from the 1954 edition, pp. 1ff). The division of grammar into two sub-types is therefore a procedural device for dealing with two intertwined aspects of language.

Thus, a morphological question about English might be: 'How is the suffix *-en* used?' An answer would include these three simplified statements:

1 It occurs in certain participial forms, like *drunken*.
2 It is inceptive in verbs like *weaken*, 'to become weak'.
3 It is causative in many such verbs, as in *weaken*, 'to make weak, to cause to become weak'.

A completely different question might be asked, of a syntactic nature, such as: 'How is causation handled in English?' Among the answers would be these simplified statements about certain suffixes:

1 Added to certain adjectives, *-en* is causative, as in *weak* / *weaken*.
2 Added to certain other adjectives, *-ify* is causative, as in *pure* / *purify*, 'to make pure'.
3 Added to certain other adjectives and some nouns, *-ize* or *-ise* is causative, as in *regular* / *regularize*, 'to make regular', and *atom* / *atomize*, 'to turn into things like atoms'.

Using these sets of examples, the relationship between form and function (morphology and syntax) can be shown diagrammatically, with regard to the suffix *-en*, as:

form   *function*

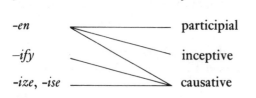

-en	participial
-ify	inceptive
-ize, *-ise*	causative

These relationships indicate the complexity of language, and also show that the answers one gets depend very much on the kind of questions one asks. It is clear, however, from this that a 'grammar' of English could be written either from a purely formal side or a purely functional side, producing a very different finished product in each case. Better, however, might be a grammar written from both points of view, as Jespersen sought to do.

2.9   The chain–choice relationship

In recent times, many linguistic theories of grammar as well as teaching methodologies have rested upon a distinction of 'chain' and 'choice', also commonly known as 'the syntagmatic and paradigmatic relations in language'. These relations were implicit in classical grammar, but are now studied and used explicitly for many purposes.

Basically, the idea of 'chain' and 'choice' is simple. Since language is a linear phenomenon, its flow can be conveniently described by means of such metaphors as 'stream', 'string' and 'chain'. A sequence, however, has to consist of things fitted into the string or chain, and this constitutes one's 'choice'. Such a situation can be expressed diagrammatically as follows:

1   The cat sat on the
| floor. |
| mat. |
| table. |
| wall. |

2   The
| dog |
| cat |
| mouse |
| bird |
sat on the mat.

3   The cat
| lay |
| sat |
| slept |
| crouched |
on the mat.

4   The cat sat
| near |
| on |
| beside |
| in front of |
the mat.

5
| Our |
| The |
| This |
| That |
cat sat on the mat.

```
                    | my        |
6   The cat sat on  | the       | mat.
                    | her       |
                    | its       |
                    | the dog's |
```

All of these variations indicate a basic chain and an infinity of possible choices, together making up much of the nature of language. The chain–choice relationship is implicit in classical grammar, and has been made explicit in modern linguistics by de Saussure, Hjelmslev and others. It can be used in the description of relationships in phonology, orthography, syntax, semantics and lexicology, and is the foundation of many presentations in language teaching and learning:

```
7   bat or bat or bat      (showing contrasts in the elements of speech
     p      d     e        and writing, though sounds are, of course,
     c      n     i        usually shown in strict phonetic or
     g      ng    u        phonemic transcription)
```

```
8   partio      (an economic presentation of a verb tense in Latin; an
    is          even more economical one would not reproduce the 'i')
    it
    imus
    itis
    iunt
```

9

I	leave
you	
we	
they	
he	leaves
she	
it	

The last of these succinct devices is well known nowadays as a 'substitution table', widely used in all sorts of language courses generally considered to be in some sense 'modern', yet it will be seen to share many of the essential features of classical paradigms. Because such paradigms often in fact expressed choices or contrasts, the Danish linguist Louis Hjelmslev labelled the vertical lists as 'paradigmatic', and this term is now fully established in this role. The horizontal line, the chain, has always been the concern of syntax, and so de Saussure coined for it the name 'syntagm' or 'syntagma', and its relations are therefore 'syntagmatic'. Diagrammatically, this can be shown as:

```
paradigmatic                |
relations                   |
('choice')                  |
                            |
            _____|_____
                            |
                            |        syntagmatic
                            |        relations
                            |        ('chain')
                            |
```

Consequently, for the preceding items 1 to 9, we can say that the contents of the vertical column are in paradigmatic relationship with one another, while the contents of the horizontal column are in syntagmatic relationship with one another.

A moment's thought will reveal that these relations refer to an item's potentiality of occurrence: it *could* appear in certain slots, but it need not always do so. For parts of certain Latin verbs, particular items *must* appear at certain points, but generally – in sentences like 'The cat sat on the mat' – the presence or absence of a potential occupant of a slot will depend on a whole range of factors. Such considerations, however, lie at the base of all the blank-filling exercises and tests that have ever been created, dealing with the predictability or desirability (or whatever) of certain items in certain places. Thus, it is the easiest thing in the world, on the basis of such relations, to create something like:

10 The __?__ sat on the mat.
   A mountain   B do   C cat   D very   E new

where the function and meaning of distinct categories or classes of words are clearly demonstrated to anyone with a fair knowledge of the language, or:

11 The __?__ sat on the mat.
   A elephant   B bee   C house   D love   E cat

where differences within one category or class (nouns) can be highlighted, or:

12 The __?__ sat on the mat.
   A child   B cat   C man   D dog   E kitten

where in effect similarities within the class of nouns are presented, in a way which indeed means that no 'best' choice can be made, because there is not enough context to suggest the 'right' answer.

Paradigmatic and syntagmatic relations are therefore closely linked with what is nowadays called 'distribution'. The idea of distribution refers to the kind of linguistic contexts in which any linguistic item or items normally occur. In example 10 above, out of the words offered, only 'cat' sensibly occurs in the given context. In 11 above 'cat', 'bee' and 'elephant' are all possible, but 'cat' is more likely because of size problems and the idea, say, of bees 'sitting'. In 12 all of the items have the same potential – that is, they are said to be 'distributionally equivalent' – although 'cat' might make a special claim if, and only if, we were interested in getting a rhyme for 'sat' and 'mat'. It should be noted that such a rhyme is only possible because, in the context of letters and/or sounds, the three words 'cat', 'sat' and 'mat' are paradigmatic, with the elements 'c', 's' and 'm' being distributionally equivalent, thus:

13 cat
   s
   m

Where items are not usually equivalents (that is, where they do not potentially share the same paradigmatic slots), then we say that they are 'in complementary distribution', and such distribution is essentially syntagmatic. That is, in 'The cat sat on the mat', the six items complement each other in creating a meaningful chain. In effect, the vertical relationship is one of lists, while the horizontal relationship is one of links, to create new communicative chains.

It is important, however, to note that syntagmatic relationships are not always strictly sequential: they can and do sometimes occur out of sequence. A simple example of this can be taken from the graphic medium, in the spelling of certain English words. Consider the following two items:

14 tal
   tale

In each of these, when pronounced, there is a vowel in mid-position between two consonants. In writing, however, there are two 'vowels' in the second item. The second vowel is traditionally called 'mute', but its *real* value is to change the phonetic realization of the first vowel. In other words, the information about the pronunciation of the spoken vowel in 'tale' is carried not on one letter but two, and these two letters are not in strict sequence, but are separated by a third letter. Such purely visual relationships allow certain distinctions to be made on paper which cannot be made in sound, such as in this pair of homophones:

15 tale
   tail

where the 'ai' combination is strictly sequential, but the 'a–e' combination is not, although their phonetic realizations are identical.

Some odd effects can be produced by the non-equivalence of speech and writing, especially when shown paradigmatically, as in:

16 tala
   tale
   tali
   talo
   talu

English can assign pronunciations to each of the listed items, but – because of certain historical developments in the writing of English – the second item in the list is anomalous. Graphically, it fits; in pronunciation, it is a non-member of the group, unless a special diacritical mark is introduced to change our normal interpretation:

17 tala
   talē
   tali
   talo
   talu

in which case, in all probability, we would become convinced that we were not looking at anything English at all, but at some list from a very different language. This kind of thing is, however, very significant in such matters as the teaching of reading and writing to English-speaking children and to foreign learners of English, and can often only be adequately demonstrated by using the chain–choice relationship.

It is a simple relationship – sufficiently simple to be the necessary basic system-building fact of language.

2.10   One grammar or many grammars?

Any kind of grammatical study of a language should be distinguished from social attitudes and expectations regarding that grammatical study. Traditionally, however, grammarians have been expected to be prescriptive or normative about language usage, whereas modern linguistics is fundamentally a descriptive and explanatory study.

Alongside the purely theoretical study of grammar there seems always to have been a belief that, somehow, the grammarian can get at the 'truth' about a language, and thereby lay down the law for others to obey. This belief is particularly strong where a powerful standard form of a language has developed, with an accompanying 'classical' literature to which people refer for inspiration and guidance of any kind. In consequence, the idea of the grammarian as legislator is a very powerful idea in most if not all literate societies.

The idea of legislating for a language, of 'fixing' it against the ravages of time and the barbarians, is also linked with the view that a language has – or had at some time in the past – a 'pure' form. As we have seen, the Greek Stoics believed this, and for political reasons many other groups have asserted it as an element in, say, some nationalistic campaign where a language could serve to symbolize a community. Such politicizing of language is common enough, and often leads to demands for the 'purification' of that language from certain undesired elements.

Veneration for the past often figures in such ideas, reference being made to certain 'classical' or 'golden' periods when everything was better than it is now, or to a canon of excellence – a religious book or a heritage of writers which forever establishes the true and the beautiful. Frequently, an element of messianism enters into such a syndrome, so that defenders of the finest and best see themselves as working *either* to maintain the citadel against creeping or violent overthrow *or* to bring about a revival, envisioning a new golden age in the future.

For a long time, in the history of Western Europe and North America, scholars looked back wistfully either towards the ages when Latin was dominant, or to some lesser golden age, such as the Renaissance or the Enlightenment. As the European vernaculars took over from Latin and competed as imperial languages themselves, their literatures took over much of the warm glow of 'rightness' that classical Latin literature has always had. This was particularly true of Italy and France, where the importance of the written word was great and academies of 'immortal' scholars could be relied upon to supervise the standard language.

Partly because English never had an academy – although the idea was warmly debated in the eighteenth century – and partly because its structure was much less in line with Latin than the structure of the Romance languages, grammarians of English never acquired as great an authority as their French counterparts – and English literature was viewed less as a source to which one could go for 'good usage'. Shakespeare, for example, has never been seriously regarded as a guide in the writing of good English.

There are therefore differences from nation to nation as regards attitudes to literature and grammar, but it is probably fair to say that the educational systems that have developed since the late eighteenth century have all used grammar as a tool for reinforcing standard languages in states that for various reasons wanted a measure of linguistic and social homogeneity among their peoples. This is as true of the French and the British as it is true of the Germans and the Americans. To say this is not to make any judgements as to the goodness or badness of such a policy, but simply to observe that it has been so: universal education, as it has developed, appears to have needed some degree of enforced linguistic conformity. Today, many educators question the necessity of such conformity. From the strictly linguistic point of view all such matters are appropriate to sociolinguistics, worthy in themselves of study, and should be kept separate from the essential nature of grammar *per se.*

In the nineteenth century, many scholars were able for the first time to examine in detail the very different languages of such places as North America, Polynesia, Africa and Asia. Many such languages had no written form, while others had venerable written forms and approaches to grammar that were in no way inferior to the classical European tradition. Additionally, investigators examined via texts of many kinds the historical and geographical differences in languages, discovering regularities even in the changes in a language through time, becoming aware that the 'dialects' of a language were simply variants along geographical and social continuums, and not degenerate forms of a pure standard. In this way, tensions inevitably developed between the prescriptive on the one hand and the descriptive on the other – tensions which even coexist inside the same person, as he or she might choose to be impartial on some occasions but very dogmatic on others.

The twentieth century has, in consequence, been something of a battleground between two warring approaches to language: attempts to maintain a heritage and a standard, and to assert what is 'good', 'correct' and 'desirable', as against a wish to stand back and examine language and social behaviour from as objective a position as possible.

This warfare has been complicated by an additional dispute of a socio-political nature: the quasi-Marxist defence of the workers and socially dispossessed against the middle-class and the established élite. In this guerrilla warfare – often carried on in the classroom as well as the street – proponents of 'equality' have objected strongly to the imposition of 'bourgeois' norms on 'the people'. The move away from middle-class certainties has included a liberal 'permissiveness' which says that more or less anything goes in language, that one should just be oneself, that ancient traditions are for the birds. Against this, conservatives have gathered to defend 'traditional values' and among them most strongly the traditional value of prescriptive grammar.

These two quarrels often run together, and some traditionalists see linguistic scientists as being on the side of the Goths and Vandals – while proponents of permissiveness gladly use linguistic arguments where they appear to be good propaganda material for their cause. It must be stressed, however, that in principle there is no connection between the science of linguistics as such and demands for greater social and personal freedom. Linguistics has nothing directly to do with the build-up or breakdown of social norms as regards language or anything else. What non-linguistic activists seek to do with the findings of linguistic theory may well be a matter of interest to linguists and indeed some linguists may in other dimensions of their lives be social activists of one kind or another, but such matters are social, not scientific as such. Linguists do not necessarily have any say in such matters, any more than any kind of investigator necessarily has control over what society does with the results of his or her investigation, once these results have been made public.

Within the burgeoning subject of linguistics (including its sub-disciplines and the fringe of quasi-linguistic activities that surrounds it), the term 'grammar' is also undergoing further transformations far removed from its ancient classical roots.

One such transformation is the way in which we now talk of 'grammars' of a language as opposed to 'the grammar' of a language. It is considered quite legitimate in linguistics that different descriptions and models may be set up, for experimental purposes, in order to see how much and how well they describe, explain and predict. We do not have space here to go into such matters in detail; suffice it to list the theories of grammar that, in 1976, the editors of the *Encyclopaedia Britannica* chose to describe in their fifteenth edition: 'comparative grammar' (among languages); 'descriptive grammar' (in linguistics today); 'prescriptive grammar' (in earlier traditions); 'generative grammar' and 'transformational grammar' (separately entered, the two main aspects of Noam Chomsky's logico-syntactic school of linguistics); 'historical grammar' (structural change in languages through time), 'stratificational grammar' (a system of levels and networks proposed by Sydney Lamb); 'structural grammar' (as propounded by the Russians Nikolay Trubetzkoy and Roman Jakobson). Others can be added to these, such as 'contrastive grammar' (emphasizing the differences among languages) and 'systemic grammar' (as developed by Michael Halliday); the *Britannica*'s choice serves, however, to emphasize the current fluidity in the subject.

What is by and large accepted today, however, is that all such theories and approaches are limited and their results provisional. Language as a dynamic social and historical phenomenon is conceived as amenable to a variety of descriptions, all incomplete, all in some ways insightful, some better for some purposes, some better for others. Certain grammars, known specifically as 'pedagogical grammars' and usually the work of 'applied linguists', are seen as having a direct or indirect application to language teaching and learning. These come closest to the traditional prescriptive approach and may lend themselves quite often to a discussion of 'norms' and 'standards' in a way that the more theoretical constructs do not.

2.11   Primary and secondary grammar

Many linguists nowadays ask questions that were not explicitly asked by traditional grammarians. One such question is: to what extent can a descriptive grammar of a language hope to reflect the system actually present in the 'mind' or 'brain' of a user of that language? Such questions inevitably widen the whole discussion of what 'grammar' is or can be.

No attempt has been made in this survey to describe in detail the content and organization of either traditional grammar or such modern approaches as structuralism and transformationalism. Such accounts can be found elsewhere. Rather, the emphasis has been on demonstrating continuity, on outlining an on-going tradition that is at least twenty-five centuries old.

Human beings, it would seem, are innate organizers. They will seek out order if it is anywhere present; if it is not present, they will create it, and if it is not sufficiently present they will impose more of it (if they can). This, as we have seen, was true of the analogists in ancient Alexandria. It is also true of the sense organs of every single one of us. The eye, for example, will contrive to see certain patterns where such patterns are not in fact present – or, like computers, may enhance a pattern that is in some way incomplete.

Grammar is just one consequence among many of this urge towards finding order in, or imposing order on, natural phenomena. It has therefore had both an order-seeking (descriptive–explanatory) aspect, and an order-imposing (prescriptive–normative) aspect. Since this is so, it is not unreasonable to assume, as many of the ancients as well as many linguists today seem to agree, that a great deal of such order is already actually present in language – in the un- and semiconscious ease with which people handle their native speech forms. Certainly, we see very clearly that order is essential in writing. The existence of such things as paradigmatic and syntagmatic relations implies that language is, by and large, a naturally orderly phenomenon. It is a system; we do not impose imaginary orderliness upon it. This might be said to be obvious; in the sense that we are clearly language-using beings we must therefore have an encoding and decoding apparatus in our heads. But the idea that we grow up with a natural internal grammar has by no means always been obvious, and where it may have been apparent, it has not always been regarded as desirable, since many extreme prescriptivists have been ready and waiting to replace it with something else. It is also by no means obvious that the natural language system in our heads is the same as our descriptions of it. All the descriptions made from Plato's day to this could be quite erroneous as regards how things proceed in our brains. We think we know what we mean by 'words' and 'sentences', but such terms may only vaguely approximate to the neural reality inside our heads.

That neural reality is both individual and shared: we have our private versions of public language, and, conversely, there is a public consensus that allows communion between a mass of private languages with their private organizations (our idiolects), in which everyone is his or her own grammarian and legislator. Viewed from this angle, it is amazing that we achieve as much agreement as we do, but not surprising that everybody has some kind of objection to, and doubts about, everybody else's way of using a language.

The grammar inside our heads, because it operates subliminally – at least most of the time – is not easily amenable to analysis. No one can as yet in any sense open up a human head and observe the functioning of language; until the time when (if ever) this can be done, we have to rest content with personal introspection and interpersonal discussion and comparison, preferably without assumptions of superiority on one side or the other as regards usage. Ultimately, all grammatical work is a search for agreement about the appropriate intelligible use of language in the various situations of life. There is evidence to suggest, in our general experience, that an awareness of language – a fully conscious appreciation of how things can be put together and used – improves over time the skills of an interested performer, but we do not have any reliable means of quantifying such things at the moment.

In a broad sense, all language can be called 'artificial', in that it is a social artifact and not a product of nature. There are, however, two levels to this artificiality: firstly, a basic level which is largely non-conscious (but not as unconscious and autonomic as, say, the flowing of our blood); secondly, there is a cultural level, largely the product of literacy, in which people can consciously examine language in general and their own use of language in particular. Diagrammatically, this can be shown as:

grammar
generally
— primary or natural grammar
[non-conscious or subliminal]

— secondary or analytical grammar
[conscious and cultural]

Primary grammar exists to facilitate actual performance; it is, in Chomsky's words, an underlying competence. It is 'rule-like' behaviour that promotes communication, and in my own view tempts us into seeing it as 'rule-governed', although it is as much governed by tendencies as by hard-and-fast rules. Secondary grammar is, by contrast, the product of a self-analysing civilization and is (as we have seen) in its turn of two kinds, so that the simple diagram above can be extended as follows:

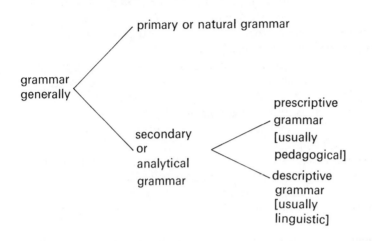

grammar generally

primary or natural grammar

secondary or analytical grammar

prescriptive grammar [usually pedagogical]

descriptive grammar [usually linguistic]

The model suggests separateness, as all such tree- or container-like models do, but in fact we can suppose a constant interplay among the three parts, conditioned by the capacity, attitudes, knowledge and needs of the persons concerned with any or all three at any time.

Having come this far, it may now be possible to go back, with a degree of enlightenment, to reconsider the twelve sentences presented at the start, each of which used the term 'grammar' in a different way. We can repeat each now with a brief comment that will serve as a kind of résumé of the survey:

1   'Grammar is the rules people use when speaking or writing a language.' This sentence remains a good general statement of fact, but we have seen that originally grammar developed as an analysis of the written language, and that the idea of 'rules' developed out of an original idea of 'analogies' at work in language. Additionally, one's attitude to the concept 'rule' will be different if one is thinking prescriptively and traditionally from the occasions when one is thinking linguistically and descriptively. Prescriptively, a rule is imposed from outside, by an authority who 'knows best'. Descriptively, rule-like phenomena are discerned in language behaviour, operating as part of the user's personal underlying competence.

2   'He bought a new French grammar.' This is, of course, a transfer from the general use of the word to the container for the grammar, in this instance a book. Nowadays, the idea can be extended to other kinds of containers, such as a human brain or a computer databank. 'How many grammars are there in the computer?' is a possible modern question.

3 'She corrected his bad grammar.' This is a common usage, and could be either pedagogical or linked with social preferences. The sentence could refer either to someone helping a foreign learner or a child; it could also refer to someone trying to alter the dialect of another person towards a socially preferred form. The presence of the adjective 'bad' suggests social disapproval.

4 'The wizard was busy with grammar and other strange doings.' At first sight this was probably the strangest of the twelve sentences; not surprisingly, since the usage is obsolete. Nonetheless, we have seen that for many centuries grammar was linked in the popular mind with occultism, and echoes of this old attitude, especially towards 'book learning', still exist today.

5 'The boys went to a local grammar school.' Here, the reference is to a certain type of school, particularly common in England, where students received a general education which was, however, firmly based in earlier centuries upon a knowledge of the grammar of Latin.

6 'That language was never written down, so it doesn't really have a grammar.' This kind of statement goes straight back to the ancient Greek interest in written language, suggesting that – somehow – a spoken language is chaotic or unordered. In the sense that no written form exists of the language in question, and that therefore no analysis of that written language exists, the statement is true. In the sense that because there is no written form therefore there can be no true orderliness in the language, the statement is false.

7 'English is a language that doesn't have much grammar.' This frequently-expressed opinion essentially views the structure of English from the point of view of Latin or some similarly inflected language. In the sense that English grammar is not Latin grammar, it is in a way true; in ultimate terms, referring to language structure, it is nonsense.

8 '"Grammar" and "syntax" are really the same thing.' By and large, people use these two terms as rough synonyms, but, as we have seen, the term 'syntax' can usefully be contrasted with a third term, 'morphology'. Syntax relates to function, while morphology relates to form. It is probably safer, therefore, to regard 'syntax' as a subdivision of 'grammar'.

9 'People who know a language work from grammars inside their heads.' This sentence relates to the modern idea that there is a natural grammar as well as an analytical and conscious grammatical description. 'Grammar' here means a neural system organized for language, and in this sense is incontrovertible.

10 'The grammar of a language includes how to spell it and pronounce it.' This kind of statement may or may not be true, depending on

how one chooses to define 'grammar'. Some people *do* use the term in the wide sense that all organizational facts about a language are part of its grammar. Others, including most modern linguists, would say that spelling relates to the special and distinct organization of the graphic medium, and pronunciation to the phonic medium. Such matters may – and often do – have grammatical relevance, but need not be handled within grammar as such, which deals with basic linguistic organization, regardless of which medium is being used.

11 'Descriptive grammar is very different from prescriptive grammar.' Probably the most important difference is that prescriptive grammar is usually conceived as a monolith, a single 'true' account of 'good usage', whereas descriptive grammar is multifarious and provisional, assuming an indefinite number of possible – better or worse – descriptions and explanations of how a language works.

12 'Traditional grammar and modern theories like transformational–generative grammar both seek to describe and explain natural language.' This last statement is probably true. The Greeks sought long ago to describe and explain language – via its written form and the 'best' poets and prose-writers, etc. Similarly, but with very different emphases, modern scientific linguists are interested in understanding what language is and how it works. Such basically objective approaches may, however, be applied by others to specific ends – particularly in pedagogy and social engineering. These attempts may interest the pure theorists, and some may even become personally involved in them, but they are not the primary concern of the linguistic investigator, which is the subject for its own sake. Such applications of theory may or may not prove socially worthwhile.

In sum, the analyses and categories developed by the ancient Greeks still have a relevance today, and no linguistic theory is entirely free from their influence, while some modern movements are very deeply indebted indeed to classical assumptions about logic and syntax. In consequence, as Dinneen suggested, it can do no harm and may do a lot of good to know something of this heritage.

It may, for example, save us from believing either that 'grammar' is a permanent God-given reality or that it was only invented a few years ago.

Part 3 The gift of tongues? – A review of language teaching in its sociocultural setting

A consideration of choice (and lack of choice) in language learning, as well as the methods and approaches currently competing for the attention of language teachers, the whole discussed in relation to our educational systems and general cultural attitudes towards language, language teaching and language learning.

Truly successful teachers are highly idiosyncratic. From this plethora of information and recommendations they select. They take from the new what suits their own personality and their teaching style and what is appropriate for the personalities and aspirations of their students, thus forming their own approach. They are not afraid to innovate, to rearrange, to redesign their courses, because continual reflection and appropriate adjustment and readjustment keep them professionally alive, making them more interesting to their students. Above all, they do not remain caught up in their own discipline but see it in relation to the total educational experience.

(Wilga M. Rivers, *Speaking in Many Tongues: Essays in Foreign-Language Teaching*, 3rd edition 1983, p. xi)

3.0 Introduction

The teaching of languages is nowadays a service industry. All over the world, the teaching of 'first', 'standard', 'second', 'foreign' or 'alternative' languages proceeds on an unprecedented scale. More time, money, effort and physical resources are being directed towards formal work on languages than ever before in human history. Indeed, so many people are now involved in this industry that putting them suddenly out of work would significantly affect unemployment figures for the middle classes in many nations. It has been said that the majority of all the scientists who have ever lived are alive and at work today. That is probably also true for the world's language teachers.

A long and interesting essay could be written on the reasons for this. Such an essay would discuss the dream of 'universal education', and the place in such an education of language training, of the skills of listening and speaking, reading and writing. It would sketch the great social changes of the last two hundred years, including the revolutions, and it would probably say quite a lot about the intercourse of nations, about translation, travel, commerce and many other things which now operate on a planetary scale. Such descriptions of trends would be interesting and useful, but somewhere along the line the individual teacher and the individual student would get lost in the statistics and the global perspective.

Somehow, nonetheless, one has to be able to reconcile the macrocosm and the microcosm – the vast drift of nations, the conflict of policies, the schemes for the education of millions, the decisions of remote ministries, all of these against the everyday realities of teacher, student and class. They must, somehow, be reconciled, because they are aspects of the same thing. Books on language teaching and learning often by-pass the larger issues in order to concentrate on classroom minutiae. The immediate details of teaching are attractive because they seem so much more manageable and human-sized than the grand themes, but both aspects have, ultimately, to go together – if only because the teacher works at the point where macrocosm and microcosm meet.

The language teacher looks outward towards the enormous complexities of educational politics on the one hand and the nature of the community that speaks the language that he or she teaches. Simultaneously, the same teacher looks inward towards one or more students who have to be guided into a working ability in that language, despite its complexities and the flux of life. This survey seeks to look at some of the problems that confront such a teacher, every day of his or her working life.

3.1   Choice and our language(s)

The reasons people learn certain languages are not necessarily the reasons that language enthusiasts give. Very few people have a free choice about the languages they will study or even the languages that they will refuse to study.

As regards the so-called 'mother tongue' our absence of free choice is so glaringly obvious that we often fail to see it. We are so intimately involved with our first language that it is hard to appreciate – that is, *really* appreciate emotionally as well as intellectually – that it is quite simply an accident of sociobiology that we are users of that language. We are happy users of, say, Dutch – but it might just as easily have been Danakil. We never ever had the choice.

Nowadays, by and large, we have no choice about going to school, and in school we have no choice but to follow the language policy pursued there. We learn the writing system that accompanies our spoken first language and we learn it and other things in a way that suits the authorities of the state to which we belong (again, quite by accident). In the European languages, for example, we learn to write on the line and from left to right; if history had worked differently, we would have hung the letters from the line instead, as they do in India – or would have worked from right to left, as the Arabic script is written. And it would all have been perfectly normal.

As regards foreign languages, much the same applies. Would a Scottish secondary school gladly accommodate a thirteen-year-old who passionately wanted to learn Japanese? Language enthusiasts often extol the acquisition of another language because it 'broadens the mind', 'helps one understand the mother tongue better', 'is useful when travelling', 'is culturally valuable' or 'allows a person to read great literature in the original language'. As a language enthusiast I put such arguments forward myself, but I hesitate to ascribe them to the hundreds of thousands of people of all ages and backgrounds who are currently studying a second language. The facts of life suggest, rather, that the reasons for studying a second language are essentially as follows:

1 The government, community or educational institution has decreed that a young person will experience a certain kind of education, a package containing a sub-package labelled 'the foreign language X'. For a variety of reasons certain educational managers have made this decision, and there is no appeal against it.

2 An individual discovers that, in order to succeed in a certain ambition, a certain body of knowledge is needed. This also contains a sub-package labelled 'the language X'. How that language came to be important for a certain occupation is irrelevant; it simply has to be learned. If it turns out to be interesting in itself, or interestingly taught, that is a windfall, but it is also irrelevant; it simply has to be learned.

(The language in question need not be a living language and the expertise need not be total. Thus, for many decades Latin has been an entry requirement for various European medical schools, because 'a physician needs to know Latin'. Consequently, the would-be doctor learns just enough Latin to get by. Similarly, at the beginning of the twentieth century, German was an important language for scientific publication. Young non-German scientists were consequently required to have a good reading knowledge of scientific German. In India today, many people acquire English as a 'library language', but do not speak it; others speak it a great deal in their occupations, but never use it at home, and may not read it at all as a pastime.)

3 A family may have a vested interest in language or a language, just as it may have a special interest in tennis, skiing or music. The children

of that family will receive a special kind of exposure to languages other than the first language, especially if there is anything approximating to bilingualism in the family. Such children, however, do not make the real choices about language; their parents do.

4 An individual, a family or a group may have some special incentive towards a particular language. It may have religious significance, be the original language of immigrants but no longer spoken much in the family, or may be the language of friends in another country. In such cases there could well be a social impetus towards studying that language.

5 Lastly, and for a relatively small number of people, there is the intellectual–cultural adventure, an interest in language for its own sake as well as in particular languages. As a proportion of the world's population such language enthusiasts are few in number, but taken all together they make up a significant minority, comparable to such other minorities as, say, the health enthusiasts who sustain the world's medical services and health clubs. Like all such minorities, they easily assume that their values and interests are shared by the community at large – or *ought* to be. This is an important point, because the development of language programmes is usually placed in the hands of such enthusiasts.

These five categories are not, of course, mutually exclusive; one person could belong to all five. They indicate clearly enough, however, that freedom of choice is limited. It might be supposed, however, that, although choice is limited as regards choosing a language to learn, it is free as regards deciding not to co-operate. Certainly, free will is involved in opting out, but it is also subject to various collective pressures upon the individual, much as follows:

1 The learner may belong to a massively unilingual community, like England or the traditional United States. In such an environment, it is hard, especially for a young person, to believe that French or German is really useful. Social motivation is effectively nil, so opting out requires no great effort.

2 The home language has already shaped both mind and mouth, and interferes with the acquisition of any alternative system, which is a kind of competition. The strangeness of the second language makes it suspect, and pressure from awkward and unconvinced peers can prevent even linguistically talented individuals from making a real effort. As in (1), social inertia and conformity are on the side of the dropout.

3 The educational programme may, for a variety of reasons, not do a very satisfactory job on the mother tongue. Someone who is already having problems in the home language is unlikely to want to take on

more problems. Opting out here is the result of accumulating linguistic failures in a language the student is already supposed, in some sense, to *know*.

4 The educational programme may, for a variety of reasons, not do a very good job as regards the second language, and consequently the student can link the boredom or dissatisfaction of the work with the target language itself.

5 There may be sociopolitical reasons why the target language is actually unpopular in the learner's community; certain people might actively urge the student *not* to learn that language. The reasons for this could be nationalistic, could relate to a real or assumed cultural colonialism, a recent imperial relationship (where the second language was the imperial language), or the language could belong to present or past enemies. It could therefore be construed as 'unpatriotic' to do well in learning that language.

6 There may also be a whole spectrum of obvious or covert reasons why someone finds the second language difficult. Influential factors here might be lack of cultural stimulation, level of intelligence, poverty, class, neurosis, physical or mental handicaps, family background and so on. In some cases, such problems might be amenable to therapy of one kind or another, if it is available, in others they might not.

Given the complexity of factors governing the availability of certain languages and the likelihood of their rejection, it is a pleasant surprise that, in fact, teachers of languages achieve as much as they *do* achieve around the world. Many people make it into fluency in a second language, and are glad of it, despite the travail involved. When all is said and done, even the most parochial person has a certain admiration for people who can perform in another language. This is a very ancient response, and may often be tinged with suspicion ('What are they saying about me?'), but it is *real enough*. The game is ultimately worth the candle.

3.2 Survival and success in language teaching

The same factors govern the teaching of languages as govern the teaching of anything else. Such factors include: national and local attitudes to education; the ideological and physical nature of the institution where the teaching takes place; and the morale, skill and humanity of the teachers themselves.

Teaching is an art. As an art, much of it is idiosyncratic, a personal achievement of the teacher. A capable teacher can take the dullest material and give it life, and an incapable teacher can denude the finest material of all interest. A flexible, dynamic and caring educational system can make even poor teachers produce good results. A rigid, static and doctrinaire educational system, or a system whose constituents are at war with each other, can render futile the best work of its best teachers.

Some makers of educational materials, cynical about the quality of the world's teachers, have tried to produce 'teacher-proof' materials, organized so that even the worst and least-informed instructor can't get it wrong. There is a kind of pragmatic wisdom in this, given the wide variations in teaching skills throughout the world, but ultimately education stands or falls by the quality of the persons to whom the work is entrusted, and not the quality of the aids, however important these may be. However good the materials are, however shiny the technology, the human guide remains central.

Nothing that is taught can be isolated from the sociocultural matrix in which it occurs. National policies, cultural attitudes, political disputes, class tensions, economic differences – all of these and other factors walk into the classroom with the students and the teacher, stay there throughout the lesson, and go out again with them at the end.

Nothing that is taught can be isolated from the surroundings in which the work is done, though an inspiring teacher can compensate for all sorts of deficiencies in accommodation, furniture, fittings, lighting, heating and the like. The way in which an educational institution functions affects the quality of the work done there, and the sheer physical shape of the place will also leave its mark on everybody who works there. Timetables, work periods, breaks, homework policy, access to books and equipment, room size and shape, windows, décor, seating, lighting, heating, recreation, canteens, unions, clubs, tests, certificates and so on – all these and more will affect the outcome of whatever teaching is done. Education is the product of a dynamic equilibrium among innumerable sociophysical factors, and its success is measured by the way the pluses and minuses work out for each individual.

On the human level, among teachers and students alike in any institution there develops a network of interpersonal relations: friendships and enmities or indifference, rivalries and intrigues or opting out, enthusiasms, jealousies, stresses and strains of all kinds, kinds of gratitude, kinds of resentment and so on, all producing the endless soap opera of school, college and university life that may mean more to some people than the actual business of teaching and learning.

Many discussions of teaching methodology by-pass these factors, because the authors feel that they are either too obvious or too general or too hard to handle – yet they crucially influence classroom progress and can make nonsense of the most delicately planned new methodological approach.

They make up the pluses and minuses of real life, and may decide whether a person continues to teach or to study, quite regardless of the subject itself and any personal enthusiasm for it.

These are all factors which externally influence the morale of the teacher one way or the other. Many of them – such as national educational decisions taken at government level – are quite beyond the individual's power to alter in any way. They may be satisfactory or unsatisfactory factors, and the individual teacher needs a mechanism to cope with such things, as well as the day-to-day affairs of the institution and the day-to-day demands of classwork and the students. The following list is usually put forward (in one form or another) as a set of recommendations about 'the good teacher'. It is certainly that, but I would also like to put it forward as a means whereby the teacher can acquire a certain armour against the slings and arrows of life – the armour of professionalism. From time to time I have asked groups of teachers whether they see themselves as 'professionals', and often a certain wistfulness enters into the discussion. Child-minders, yes, maybe even civil servants, and trade unionists too, and often social scapegoats – but professional, in the way that doctors and lawyers are professional? That, for many, seems too much to hope for.

The matter of self-motivation and self-discipline

Although these are constantly affected by outside factors, they can nevertheless have a surprising autonomy, as described in the old adages 'do it for its own sake' and 'if a thing is worth doing, it's worth doing well'. Essentially – and unsentimentally – this is the pride that craftsmen take in their work, despite whatever the world does: the face will be carved despite the grain of the wood, the right colour will be found for the sky. In theatrical circles, it is the same attitude of mind as in 'the show must go on'. In its most extreme form, it is like the army doctor who goes on patching up bodies while others go on blowing them to pieces. Education has its heroisms too.

The craft of teaching demands certain standards that are internally imposed, not externally required. The external requirements about when a teacher will teach are clear enough, but just how the teacher manages all the elements relating to running an actual class is a matter of personal control – and pride. One example might suffice to illustrate this. From time to time a competent teacher may be seduced by his or her own eloquence and the interest of the class – and run over the time-limit, or concentrate too long on one area of the syllabus. Self-control is vital here, to limit the damage that can be caused by this over-enthusiasm, avoiding, say, the last-minute rush necessary to complete the syllabus in good time for an external test.

Enthusiasm for the work

Motivation and discipline shade into enthusiasm for the work. Such enthusiasm is infectious, and often, when other forms of motivation are not strong in the students, they will learn quite simply because the teacher is enjoying the job. In a real sense, enthusiasm precedes knowledge, because it can lead to knowledge, but knowledge without enthusiasm is not easily passed on.

Interest in the student

Some teachers make it clear quite quickly – either explicitly or implicitly, in their behaviour – that research or administration or the book interests them more than the students. This is particularly the case at institutes of higher learning, where the system often encourages research work at the expense of teaching. Those who prefer the subject to the students should not teach. It is as simple as that.

Sound knowledge of the subject

From time to time a teacher can be in a situation where, for a variety of reasons, he or she is unfamiliar with the subject and is reading just ahead of the class. Emergencies can create this kind of situation, but as a general rule such teaching is stressful and dishonest; in order to succeed, the teacher may feel constrained to pretend a knowledge that he or she just does not have. The students are seldom deceived. If the teacher has the confidence and the good humour to admit this imperfect knowledge, then invites everybody to join in a common learning experience ('Let's learn this stuff together'), then something worthwhile could emerge – but, generally, a teacher who is only a little ahead of the students is a source of mutual demoralization.

'A sound knowledge of the subject' is, however, a relative matter, and teachers should retain a sense of proportion about it. A good primary school language specialist does not need the skills of a secondary school teacher (and, indeed, needs other skills). A good secondary school teacher or private tutor or teacher in a school for adults does not need to be a language academic. Each should feel competent in his or her own level and speciality, and this competence and confidence arises out of a kind of on-going love affair with the subject, a steady development in one's contact with it, regardless of whether new insights can be instantly used in a particular class or not.

Concern for the attention span of the students and for variety in the work-style of the group

No one can concentrate indefinitely, and concentration has its peaks and troughs. Many lessons are, however, given in a way that puts too heavy a strain on the capacity to pay attention and asks people to centre for too long on one kind of voice, one person in one position, one mode of delivery, and so on. The classical university lecture is just such a situation and in many instances is stimulus-deficient. To work well, it needs a skilled performer with much of the virtuosity of an actor who specializes in monologues. Such a person will use many tricks to vary an otherwise restricted programme, so that the audience won't switch off. Adults, of course, have longer attention spans than children – but not all that much longer. Smaller children need a change of direction every five minutes or so under normal conditions; many adults flag after fifteen minutes of exposure to one sense-source, unless it is very interesting indeed. When the mind wanders, however, members of an audience often feel guilty, blaming themselves because they 'haven't learned to concentrate'. Often it would have been better if the teacher had learned how to ride the patterns of concentration of the students, allowing them to manage the flow of experience better.

3.3   A model for the language classroom

In any classroom or learning situation there are, as it were, three 'components': a teacher, some students, and some kind of material to work with. How these components are associated in the mind of the teacher has definite psychological and pedagogical consequences.

To say that there are three components and that these are 'a teacher, some students and some kind of material' is already a statement with strong implications. It is linear and it suggests the priority of one thing over another. It is, in fact, a model of how things are ordered, or should be ordered, in education. The teacher comes first, the students second, and the materials last. Every linear alteration that we care to make, however, in ordering the components alters the system of priorities, and has necessary consequences in the mind. Consider each of the following:

1 teacher – students – materials
2 teacher – materials – students
3 students – teacher – materials
4 students – materials – teacher
5 materials – teacher – students
6 materials – students – teacher

Each of these is worth a little study. Something like them is at the heart of many individual approaches to teaching, or animates whole methodologies. Thus, traditional methodology has generally emphasized the role of the authoritarian dispenser of knowledge, who instructs dutiful students with the aid of a book (style 1), or reveals the contents of a venerated book to the lucky students (style 2). A contrasting modernist approach foregrounds the students in 'open-plan' activities, learning together with the help of a teacher using various aids (style 3), or using various materials while the teacher hovers here and there in the role of a resource person (style 4). In certain other situations, such as military training, there is a job to be done with certain kinds of equipment and the instructor is there to ensure that certain learners will be able to do the work (style 5), and such skills might be approached in a kind of immersion procedure with the teacher there simply to limit mistakes (style 6).

The permutations have their defenders and opponents. Presented in isolation they represent a tendency rather than an absolute style, but even so some people will find them repugnant because of their linearity. They may prefer something like the following, instead:

7 | teacher
  | students
  | materials

where the paradigmatic presentation is intended to remove the idea of linearity and one is not meant simply to read the list downwards. The implicit message here is: 'We all matter equally, you, me and the book, regardless of impressions to the contrary.' Such a style has pleasing overtones of democracy about it. To its proponents it is relaxed and humane; to its detractors it is a kind of anarchic free-for-all.

To seek out a balance, however, where there is neither psychological linearity nor any suggestion of chaos, yet another model can be proposed, one that allows any one of the three components to be foregrounded or backgrounded at any time, depending on need:

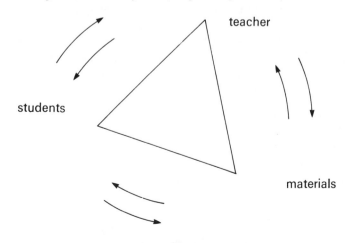

In this approach, no component can be permanently dominant. Instead, each is free to rotate into primary position, and the whole may, for example, be linked with the concept of attention span and the need for variety. For certain purposes, the teacher can perform in front of the class, at other times the materials (films, pictures, tapes, etc.) can be foregrounded, and at other times the students can (individually, in groups, in dialogues, singing or whatever) take over the classroom – everything subject to time, place, numbers, personality, goals and the like. Certainly, the teacher need not always be in the forefront of the learning process, and if he or she is in the background, there is also no need to feel guilty about it, or that a passing colleague might think that one is not earning one's salary.

A model is only an aid, a descriptive device. In the eight models presented here there is nothing of ultimate truth, but there are pointers to various attitudes and practices, explicit or implicit. Clarity of mind about such things can do no harm, and may even do some good.

3.4   A language teacher's attitudes

Every teacher inevitably brings a personal view of life into the classroom, a view that interpermeates with the work. The teacher may not always be fully aware of the effects of this fact, and it can be useful to examine its implications.

Generally speaking, trainee teachers and teachers taking refresher courses are not asked to consider the wide philosophical implications of being a teacher. Apart from exhortations to be diligent, sympathetic, fair and slightly impersonal even when friendly (for the sake of self-preservation), teachers are usually invited to concentrate on the subject itself, either in its theoretical or its practical aspect. All of these are important, but social background is also important. A teacher's worldview or 'ideology' – if that is not too strong a term – is probably not much discussed because the matter is too delicate, dangerous or divisive, but it is there nonetheless.

To demonstrate this, I will take two terms out of the preceding paragraph – 'theoretical' and 'practical'. Everyone is familiar with these terms, and we all reckon we know what they mean. In a general sense, of course, we do, but it will do no harm to re-express them as a very simple model of how the terms are often used in the profession:

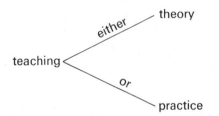

This model implies that there are two distinct and contrastive aspects to teaching. It allows such statements as: 'Well, in theory that sounds great, but in practice it doesn't work', or 'Theory is all very well, but...', or 'It's fine to have your head in the clouds, but some of us have to do the actual teaching...', and so on. Everyone makes comments like this from time to time, out of frustration or cynicism; the regular use of such comments, however, is usually coupled with an unwillingness to study the theory of a subject, and an impatience to get on with 'real' matters.

There is a quaint illogic, however, about such a view. The statement 'Theory is all very well, but...' is itself a kind of theory; it is, among other things, a generalizing statement, and generalization is an important part of theory-building. Additionally, where practice differs from a 'theory', then it is serving the purposes of theorizing, because it is serving to test – and perhaps to disconfirm – that theory. Properly handled, the practical observations could contribute to the rebuilding of the theory on a firmer foundation, or the construction of an alternative and better theory. The fact that in practice a particular theory does not work does not damn all theorizing. Everybody, all the time, builds theories.

This section, however, is not a discussion of theory and practice as such. Rather, these terms have been used to show that every professional teacher has some kind of personal viewpoint about them, and about many other things, as part of his or her personal worldview. Along with this worldview goes a cognate pattern of behaviour, and for present purposes the combination can be expressed as:

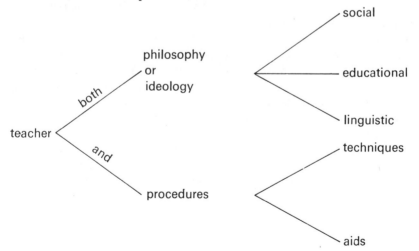

In this model, the elements are not seen as being in competition, as they were in the theory–practice model. Instead, they are points taken arbitrarily from the continuum of things. One's ideology shades into one's behaviour, and one's social attitudes flow into one's educational and linguistic attitudes.

The most extreme and obvious forms of 'philosophy' or 'ideology' will be found in nations, communities or institutions where a certain body of doctrine and dogma has to be passed on to the people, the next generation, the students or whatever. This can be religious, as in church schools, or political, as in socialist educational systems. In addition to such collective stances, each individual has his or her own view of life. A Mormon, for example, will not drink coffee and this could be noted at break times, while a Jehovah's Witness will consider that the end of this world is not far away, and proceed accordingly. Such things have subtle effects. If, for example, one person is convinced that another is not going to go to heaven, then this must inevitably affect any relationship that the two are going to enter into. If one person believes that work is worship, but another considers that leisure is the true aim in life, communion may be possible, but it will have its limitations.

A person's attitudes are not always on the surface, open to ready inspection; they could, however, show themselves in a variety of non-conscious but very specific ways, and particularly via body language. An effort is often needed to make them conscious and examinable, either in private introspection or in group study. Not everyone, however, is willing to submit his or her value system to any scrutiny whatever, and, to make matters even more complicated, may not have a fully coherent system anyway. To talk about one's values is often an invitation to rationalize, to 'explain away' rather than to explain. Worldviews are, in principle, fuzzy at the edges and in a state of flux at the best of times, even in very dogmatic people, but it can be disconcerting to have to admit that one is not always consistent and clear about what life is.

There are many areas that one might explore, but for present purposes one area will suffice. This is the teacher's conception of his or her primary role: is a teacher a social worker who happens to teach certain subjects, or an instructor of certain skills who also happens, sometimes, to be a social worker? There is, of course, a continuum between the two extreme positions, but every teacher locates himself or herself somewhere along the line.

Many teachers certainly see themselves as 'socializers', helping students – many of whom have distinct social problems, especially in areas of great social inequality or tension. Others equally clearly see themselves as carrying the torch of knowledge, as part of a continuing intellectual adventure or profession. Both views are worthy, as is the compromise position; a teacher should, however, give some thought to the matter, and may in the process discover that things have changed over the years, as he or she steadily shifted one way or the other along the continuum. Whatever the state of affairs, it is going to affect how the teacher relates to his or her students, and to the subject taught. In the confirmed social worker, the subject is a medium through which important social work can be done; in the case of the confirmed instructor, the worth of the subject comes before social problems. In the compromise position, both have equal significance. Whichever the case may be, the point on the continuum is part of the teacher's theory of what it is to be a teacher.

3.5   Home language and target language

It is generally assumed that there is a big difference between the teaching and learning of the 'mother tongue' and the teaching and learning of a 'second language'. The distinction is not, however, as clearcut as might appear at first sight.

When we leave teaching in general to concentrate on language teaching in particular, we come across a dichotomy that is generally conceived as follows:

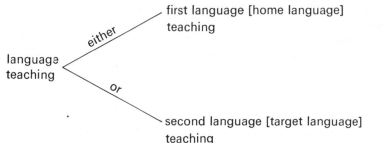

Teachers who help people develop their skills in the 'mother tongue' or home language are considered to have a very different task to perform from those who provide opportunities in another language. Books on methodology cater to each kind of teacher separately; there are few, if any, that view them as having common problems. Of course, in an important sense the general wisdom is right – the language of the home is already a living, functioning system, whereas the second language is new and may never be efficiently acquired. There are, however, some important reasons why one should not always draw too clear a line between the first and later languages. There are at least six reasons why one should be cautious in this matter:

1 It has been the custom, in European nation–states, and in others that have followed their example, to teach in the school system a standard version of a 'national' language. In the early years of education this standard form is particularly linked with reading and writing, which in its own way is a completely new language activity for the child, as new as, say, instruction in a second language. Each individual struggle towards literacy is part of a national programme aimed at linguistic uniformity.

2 Few nation–states are in any sense homogeneous. For historical rather than logical reasons their boundaries may include language minorities, or cut across whole cultural groups that then find themselves in two distinct nations. An example of the first is the presence of Breton in France; the second is exemplified by the presence of Basques in both France and Spain. This situation means that for many people the 'first' language of schooling is not the first language of the home – is not the mother tongue at all. The mother tongue may not be prestigious or linked with education and literature at all, as in many developing countries.

3 More than this, even where a nation–state has a national language that is spoken by most of its citizens, there will be great variation within the country as regards dialect. Italy, for example, is famous for the differences between *i dialetti* and the standard based on Tuscany and Dante. For many Italian children, learning the standard language is much like learning a foreign language. In many other countries, working-class children are placed in a similar situation vis-à-vis the standard, which is a middle-class creation based on a prestige dialect, perhaps originating in a now defunct royal court. England, Scotland, France, Spain and the German-speaking countries all have problems of this kind.

4 Regardless of the degree of match or mismatch between regional, class and standard dialects, the pupils are still young when they start on the standard, in either medium, and need to progress by stages through selected and graded material towards greater syntactic and semantic fluency. This is not necessarily very different from the way in which students work in a foreign language once they have moved out of the beginner stage.

5 Regardless of the language studied, certain methodological procedures of a logical nature are common to all language work. These include comprehension, question-and-answer, selection of the proper response, analysis of texts, restatement of ideas and many other techniques that inevitably appear in both kinds of language teaching.

6 'Code-switching' is a very common human activity. It means that most people can move without much effort from a style of language needed in one situation to a style needed in another. This might, within one language, mean moving from standard to slang, from middle-class to working-class, from standard to dialect, or a mix of all of these and more, as circumstances demand. It can also mean, among bilinguals, switching from one full language to another, as is done regularly in Africa and Asia, and by Hispanics in the United States. This means that the human brain can handle complex switch-over techniques, whether these relate to inside one language (say, in Quebec from 'International French' to 'joual', or in Scottish schools

from the 'classroom language' to the 'playground language') or to between languages (as in certain Welsh children using English for some purposes, Welsh for others, or Indian children who may go to English-medium schools but speak their own family language at home). These facts indicate that belief in the homogeneity of certain languages like English and French is not logical, and that in a broad but important sense we are all learning and using different kinds of language all the time.

These various points relate to regional, social, maturational and procedural facts about language that are, if we think about them, hardly contestable. Nation–states want uniformity for certain purposes, but the uniformity of the standard is only one part of the total language experience of the individual citizens. In handling the standard and any foreign language that they are exposed to, however, they face similar problems, and the ways of handling these problems are not so different. First-language and second-language teaching are not, therefore, as different as the common model suggests.

3.6 The monastery and the marketplace

In the teaching of foreign languages, we can detect two ancient traditions: 'the monastery tradition' and 'the marketplace tradition'. They are very different, and the tension between them is as strong today as ever it was, because they represent certain polarities in society.

The systematic teaching of certain languages to certain kinds of foreigners has a venerable history. It may well be as old as civilization, but we have a clear view of it only as far back as the ancient Greeks, whose basic approach was adopted by the Romans and passed on (with some embroidering) to the modern world via the medieval states of Europe. Formal language instruction within this tradition was firmly based on the written rather than the spoken word, used a system of paradigms, rules and exceptions, encouraged reading and textual analysis, and – in varying degrees over the centuries – might be supplemented by some kind of direct exposure to the spoken forms of the target language.

This general methodology – nowadays referred to, often pejoratively, as 'the grammar–translation method' – reigned largely unchallenged for over two thousand years, with its heyday from the Middle Ages into the eighteenth century. It was only towards the close of the nineteenth century, with the rise of the dream of universal education, that larger numbers of educators began to propose or invite serious alternatives to this time-sanctioned way of doing things.

One reason for the long survival of the method was the relatively slow pace of social change in a world where past values served to hold society together and were perpetuated by groups of nobles, clerics and merchants who held power. For them, in Europe and its dominions, the memory of Rome, the prestige of the Christian religion and the usefulness of both Latin and French as international languages all served to reinforce this age-old style of teaching any language.

This is not to suppose, however, that there were no other ways in which people *learned* languages. The other major 'method' was not, however, in serious competition with the grammar–translation method. It was non-academic and unstructured, the method of the marketplace rather than the monastery.

The 'marketplace' approach to language has always been dictated by simple necessity. If you want to barter, buy or sell, then you need to be able to communicate – somehow, anyhow – with your potential contacts. In the great cosmopolitan cities of history – Babylon, Alexandria, Rome, Marseilles, London, New York, and so on – the procedures of the marketplace (and the riverfront, harbour, etc.) have required practical answers to language problems. Anything that works is welcome: a go-between if possible, or gestures, pictures, your words or his words, your grammar or his grammar, or anybody's words and anybody's grammar, in order to strike a bargain. The system has always worked, but is haphazard, and gives rise to trade jargons, pidgins and creoles that are socially frowned on, much as their users – sailors, soldiers, hucksters, whores, dockers, innkeepers and, ultimately, slaves – were or are frowned on. These interlanguages are vitally alive, however, and many a respectable and matronly modern language has something of this wild blood in its family line.

The 'monastery' approach was different in every way – was, in fact, shielded from the hurly-burly of the world and its marketplaces. It abstracted its students, usually boys of an impressionable age, from the flux of everyday life and put them together in roughly homogeneous age groups for longer or shorter periods, their instructors taking on the role of stern fathers or older brothers (and, in fact, have often had the title 'father' or 'brother'). The work of instruction was in the hands of a priesthood or brotherhood such as the priests of ancient Egypt, the scribes of Babylon, the brahmins of India, the mullahs of Islam, the monks of medieval Europe, the teaching brothers and sisters of later Catholic schools and missions, the one-sex staff of semi-monastic private boarding or day schools. Much of the life of such institutions was box-like:

1 Students worked individually in cells or collectively in classrooms.
2 Their time was divided up into periods marked by the tolling of bells.
3 Strict discipline was imposed as the students learned measured doses from chaptered books.

Along with the chopped-up space and time of their lives went a system of reward and punishment and a form of indoctrination that made it clear that they were privileged people, however tough the regimen might be. Often the students went on to take holy orders themselves and might in due course instruct the next generation of learners. More and more, however, the monastic schools, colleges and universities were made available to lay-students, the children of the rich or otherwise favoured, in a social compact, and in the European states and their off-shoots such institutions served as a training ground for the children of a social élite.

This fairly stark picture hardly prevents us from recognizing the outlines of the majority of present-day schools and colleges, however much they may have mellowed in recent decades. There are, however, some important additional points to be made:

1 The Reformation, the Enlightenment, the Industrial Revolution and various other movements in recent history have nurtured such concepts as 'the work ethic' and 'universal education' with such compelling success that very few people in Western society (with one notable exception in the US flower children in the 1960s) have questioned their relevance and value in our lives. Every one of us must go to school and become literate (etc.), and then engage in productive work more or less from nine to five o'clock each weekday. Neither concept is a universal of human life, and universal education (about an equal mix of socio-economic planning and liberal humanitarianism) is still hardly a century old. Set against the million years or so of human existence on earth, it can hardly be regarded as a firmly rooted fact of life.

2 Theories of social egalitarianism, developing out of the American and French Revolutions and the writings of eighteenth- and nineteenth-century liberal and socialist thinkers, culminating in Karl Marx, have questioned the right of élites to keep prestigious forms of education to themselves (regardless of whether or not such forms would be socially useful on a large scale).

3 Economic pressures have forced educational institutions to turn more and more away from such traditional objectives as 'education for its own sake' and the training of certain kinds of people for certain professions. Today there is great official concern for the mass of humanity and for the business of making as many people as possible civilized, literate, numerate, 'technicate', and capable of earning some kind of reasonable living. Vocational objectives like these have more in common with the marketplace than the monastery. In the large state schools that draw their clientele from all or most of the families of a neighbourhood, the monastery tradition of academic excellence and abstract learning has collided head-on with social reform, politics

95

and economics. It is not really surprising, therefore, that such schools are often places of conflict among the staff and confusion among the students.

Given this abrasive coming-together of the two traditions (as part of the dream of universal education), it is surprising that so many schools and colleges do as well as they do (at least in those parts of the world without major war, revolution, famine and other troubles). Many students do become able users of both mother tongue and second language (in addition to their other school attainments). It is tempting, sometimes, to suppose that they succeed *despite* rather than because of the system; their success is a tribute as much to their human flexibility as to our institutions, which often suffer from a kind of social schizophrenia.

3.7 Methods and approaches

The teaching of foreign languages is, in the twentieth century, characterized by a number of 'methods', such methods having their fervent supporters and equally fervent detractors. New teachers often ask the 'expert' to tell them which method is the best, and, depending on his or her bias, the expert will provide an answer. Over the years, however, most authorities on teaching methodology have grown cautious about recommending the ultimate panacea; they have had their fingers burned too often. It may therefore be safer to take a relativist view of the various methods currently available, and to consider that each major approach has its strengths and its weaknesses.

The monastery tradition and the grammar–translation method were natural partners over the last eight hundred years or so, no doubt successfully resisting a variety of attempts to innovate in education, while also in their own terms achieving many marked successes. Grammar–translation methods can vary and have varied considerably in type and emphasis probably since they first acquired their characteristic features, and need not be regarded as a kind of brooding monolith presiding over centuries of frustrated students. Inspired and inspiring teachers existed then and continue to exist now, working within this tradition. The essential factor here, however, is that what is now called 'grammar–translation' was not always so labelled – it was, rather, just how things were done, and how things were done included (necessarily, it was supposed) a lot of explicit grammar and a lot of explicit translation. Many people still see these two items as essential pillars both of education and of language teaching and learning, and are in no hurry to change their minds.

Towards the end of the nineteenth century, however, there came a considerable change of attitude, a genuine revolution in the teaching of the world's languages (in formal, non-marketplace terms), and this revolution is not yet over. Rather, it could be said to have set up several on-going waves of radicalism.

Essentially, it was a move away from texts towards the every-day spoken forms of a language, inspired by such practical matters as greater international trade and travel. Because it set out to break the monopoly of the classicists it has made us aware of the very idea of different methods, that alternatives are possible within the framework largely bequeathed by the monastery tradition. When one has too many conflicting 'methods', however, as we seem to have today, language teachers can perhaps be forgiven for asking, angrily or plaintively, 'Which should I use?' or 'Which of these is best?'

In the original Greek the word *méthodos* (*meta + hodós*) is a 'way across' from one position or state to another, a means to an end, in this case the passage from ignorance and ineptitude to knowledge and competence. There have always been temptations, however, to imbue such 'ways across' with a salvationist quality, seeing one's own or a new way as *The* Way. In language teaching there have been many such 'methods' or routes to linguistic salvation: the direct method, the natural method, the psychological method, the reform method, the oral method, the audiolingual method, and so on. As the decades passed, however, and innovators learned caution, they began to replace the rather dogmatically assertive 'method' with the safer and humbler 'approach', so that we have had more recently: the structural approach, the situational approach, the communicative approach, and so on. Indeed, it is common now to see the term 'approach' as being wider and less specific than 'method', the general ideological setting within which 'methods' may develop.

Terminological distinctions apart, it is not often easy to see where one panacea ends and another begins, and indeed methods and approaches blur at times and run into each other as individuals experiment or even, let it be admitted, when they cobble materials together from different approaches without knowing that the experts fight hotly to keep them apart. The 'bandwagon effect' is also at work, where for various reasons people may climb aboard the latest bandwagon, carried away by its novelty and the enthusiasm of its proponents, but not always too clear on what they are getting into.

To try to present all the intricacies of language methodology over the last hundred years in a few pages is impossible, but, working with a broad brush on a large canvas, I may be able to paint in some important general features by means of which we can analyse courses and curricula when we meet them. The diagrammatic model that follows is a kind of overview of methods and approaches, and is followed in turn by some brief résumés of the main characteristics of each:

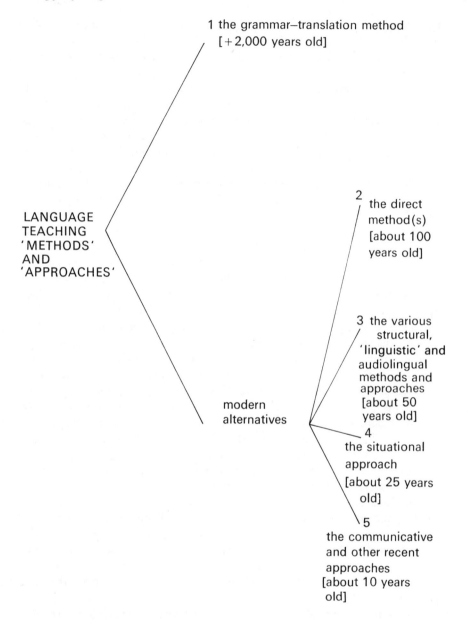

1   The grammar–translation method

Inextricably linked with the monastery tradition, this 'method' has generally taken the body of received knowledge as primary and the teacher as secondary. In essence it is the teacher's task, almost privilege, to pass on something that is already established, and to do it in an established way, using the right kind of books with the right kind of paradigms and rules, lists of regularities and exceptions, texts for guided reading and fixed exercises in two-way translation. Rote learning and application of the rules was (and is) the basic procedure, the use of examples and exercises encouraging a deductive, analytical approach to language. Additionally, because the emphasis is on a classic form of the target language expressed through canonical literary texts, the student develops his or her skills within a relatively restricted area of formal written language.

2   The direct method(s)

Late nineteenth-century innovators such as François Gouin, Wilhelm Viëtor, Otto Jespersen and Maximilian Berlitz were primarily intent on moving the focus of foreign-language teaching away from rules and literary texts towards the living (colloquial) language, arguing that speech is primary and the learning of everyday language a useful practical activity. It was supposed by such pioneers that language could be taught 'directly' (that is, without the mediation of translation) and 'naturally' (that is, in much the same way that the students had learned their mother tongues). Berlitz in particular favoured an approach called 'total immersion' in which (not unlike aspects of marketplace learning) everything is done in the target language and without the use of explicit grammar. It was assumed that the student would slowly begin to live the language simply because there was no escape from it. Visual aids, dramatizations, special gestures and other 'direct' means were encouraged so that the student through an overwhelming involvement was enticed or compelled towards fluency.

3   The various structural methods and approaches, etc.

The early direct and natural methods were highly experimental, and slowly began to shade into forms which, always emphasizing the 'oral' or 'audiolingual' aspect, nevertheless sought to provide in very pragmatic terms various aids through which students could be facilitated in their learning. Simple exposure to the target language in all its chaotic richness was seen as less valuable than appropriate patterning. Grammar and vocabulary might not necessarily be organized for the student as explicit paradigms and lists, but the material nevertheless began to take on a shape which I can characterize here as 'structure', in line with the general tendency of linguistics and anthropology at that time (the 1920s onwards).

Direct-method enthusiasts in Britain, including Harold Palmer and Michael West, were animated more by a pragmatic desire to teach efficiently than the implementation of any particular theory of language, psychology or education. They had no wish to plunge unsuspecting students straight into real-life foreign-language conditions, and therefore emphasized the need for careful and appropriate selection, gradation and presentation in language courses, in all of which the organizer and the teacher could be fully aware of the grammatical, lexical and phonetic aspects of the materials, while the student need only be concerned with practice and acquisition. Both the spoken and written mediums were important, and West in particular undertook to develop carefully graded and simplified 'structural readers' – often adaptations of the great classics of English literature – so that the oral–aural ability of the students could be reinforced in the graphic medium. Finally, here, one should emphasize that the British structural approach has consistently sought to be immediately relevant in terms of context and meaningfulness, so that the student would not feel that exercises were divorced from what one might call marketplace realities.

The parallel American movement was in some ways more complex and certainly more tightly tied in with theories of language and psychology. Sometimes in fact called the 'linguistic approach' to language teaching, it owed its name and core ideas to the 'structuralist' school of linguistics that developed first of all in Prague as part of European linguistics then as a United States phenomenon under the aegis of Leonard Bloomfield. Bloomfield, Charles Fries and Robert Lado have been major figures in the development of structuralist methods, influenced profoundly by the behaviourist psychology of Ivan Pavlov, John Watson and Burrhus Skinner. In the 1930s both structural linguistics and behavioural psychology were seeking to provide themselves with incontestably 'scientific' credentials, principally by avoiding anything that smacked of metaphysics and mentalism in the description of human behaviour. They sought objectivity, and structuralist teachers saw their graded and repetitive sentence drills, known as 'pattern practice', as scientific, offering an excellent system of learning based upon Pavlovian stimulus and response. In class, the students were provided with linked and progressive stimuli which would, it was supposed, prompt linked and progressive responses in their conditioning as learners of the target language. The assumption was that language is habit-based, and the provision of material for good habit-formation would lead to good performance not only in class but in the world at large. Great care was taken to help the students avoid making mistakes, as mistakes could be reinforced just as easily as correct responses, and become ingrained bad habits. The methodology has been linked with a number of aids such as programmed learning, teaching machines and language 'laboratories' by means of which purposeful students could steadily train themselves or be trained in the right kind of language behaviour. The listening and speaking skills were predominant in this approach, to such an extent that the whole movement has come to be known very widely as 'the audiolingual method'.

A particularly important maxim of this period, and one that is still influential among language teachers, is: 'Nothing spoken before it is heard; nothing read before it is spoken; nothing written before it is read.' This maxim emphasizes the order given to the four assumed language skills listening, speaking, reading and writing, and represents the extreme swing of the pendulum away from the standard view of the grammar–translation method. Success in training large numbers of soldiers to use foreign languages during the Second World War (where motivation was intense and immersion techniques could be firmly implemented) gave a great boost to the structuralist–behavioural approach to language teaching and learning, but in the easier environments of schools and colleges in the fifteen or so years after the war a variety of problems emerged in the use of straight-forward audiolingualism.

4   The situational approach

From their very inception the new audiolingual and structural movements sought to enliven the classroom with real-life material in their use of gestures, dialogues and other devices. This desire for realism stimulated a further wave of innovation which followed, more or less explicitly, the theory of meaning of the British linguist John Rupert Firth who stressed the importance of 'context of situation'. Material had to have meaning in relation not simply to naked and isolated words and patterns but to what people have to do and want to do in life. Audiovisual aids continued to grow in importance (developing a whole technological back-up system), and games, dramas, songs, chants and indeed *activity* rather than passivity became crucial matters. One learned best by doing things, and the things that were to be done had to be meaningful and relate to real life 'out there' beyond the classroom's box-like walls.

The term 'situation', however, is Janus-faced: there are *real* situations 'out there' and there are *simulated* situations in the classroom, embedded more or less artificially in the selected and graded material of a syllabus. The problem was how to make simulated situations resemble real situations more successfully, how to get a wooden dialogue to turn – magically – into what one would say, hear and do in a real café or hotel. Better, the problem began to be perceived as how to *avoid* simulation and get the teacher–learner ensemble to create 'authentic' and appropriate language of its own.

The result of such considerations has been interesting. Language courses in the 1960s and 70s have still tried to be as 'direct' as possible and as natural as possible in their effect despite the great artificiality of their production, and some have been conscious hybrids, such as 'structurally-controlled situational teaching' (L. G. Alexander, *New Concept English*, 1967). This course even permits a modicum of translation, to speed up explanations and obviate the need for complex miming and paraphrase in the target language. A kind of eclecticism began to emerge, where a teacher could make a choice among the options available, and people began to show less inclination to be fanatical over the merits of one method and the demerits of all the others. On both sides of the Atlantic, specialists in language teaching have gone on proposing more and more realism in the classroom, in terms of learners' needs, which in effect means a further move away from the monastery towards the marketplace.

5 The communicative approach

Implicitly or explicitly, ever since the 'direct' revolution began, teachers have known that their aim was to get students communicating successfully outside the classroom. Recently, however, increasing attention has been paid to analysing the notion of 'communication' in order to build syllabuses and courses around whatever components it may have. One virtue of this movement has been the coming together of practitioners from both sides of the Atlantic in the desire to find common solutions to shared problems. Inspired in part at least by the sociolinguist Dell Hymes's view that we must study 'communicative competence' at least as zestfully as we have been studying linguistic competence in the abstract, theorists such as J. L. M. Trim, David Wilkins and Henry Widdowson have developed, variously, such approaches as 'notional–functionalism' and the 'communicative approach'.

These fields overlap and suffer from a degree of terminological confusion. They share, however, three significant elements:

1 an enthusiasm for language in *use* rather than language as *structure*;
2 a consequent preference for 'semantics' (meaning in real-life contexts) over 'grammar' (rules and paradigms in isolation from authentic language use) in the formulation of tasks for learners to perform;
3 an interest in analysing, and planning for, the genuine needs of the learner (an activity technically described as 'needs analysis' and taken to be an essential first step in preparing 'communicative' curricula or syllabuses).

'Notional–functionalism' concerns two general concepts of how language is used: 'notions' and 'functions'. 'Notions' relate to how we cut up the world into such things as time, space, location, movement, shape, emotions, attitudes and the like; 'functions' would appear to relate to whether at any time we want to make, describe, move, change, etc., any thing as part of the situations in which we find ourselves. An increasingly popular instance of this is how many ways there may be of indicating to someone that we want a door opened or closed: 'Close the door, please, John', 'Um, John, the door', 'The door's open, John', and so on. The 'communicative approach' is very similar if not essentially the same thing, where courses are organized in terms of such realities as giving and exchanging information, asking questions, giving orders, apologizing, confirming something, contradicting someone, and so forth.

Communicative studies form only the latest phase in the creation of a considerable literature relating to language-teaching methodology, providing another useful perspective from which we can consider the predicament of both teacher and student. It becomes increasingly difficult, nonetheless, to keep the various strands of the methodological skein apart. This is especially so in training newcomers to the business of second-language teaching and (in in-service refresher courses) preventing some established teachers from throwing up their arms in despair at the quantities of stuff vying for their attention. There is certainly a danger that, in areas where approaches, policies and materials change completely almost every two years a kind of professional burnout will occur: the arrival of the latest panacea may prove to be the arrival of one panacea too many.

We do not as yet have a respectable and comprehensive theory of either how people learn in general or how they learn languages in particular, although enthusiasts sometimes give the impression that we have, or very nearly have. Until we get such a theory (if ever), we will not have the means of substantiating our pet techniques or disconfirming those that are anathema to us. The matter is not yet properly 'scientific', and it may even be wrong-headed to insist that it ever should become properly scientific. The accomplished teacher works as much by 'feel' as by the rational application of well-researched method – as does the accomplished artist in any field – and by and large we can only speculate and tell anecdotes to account for why this is so.

3.8 Conservatives and radicals in the classroom

In addition to a historical examination of the five major language-teaching methods (grammar–translation, direct, structural, situational and communicative), the whole question of methodology can be usefully examined at the present time by looking at an individual teacher's attitudes and techniques. Such attitudes and techniques can be described as polarizing between 'conservative' and 'radical' positions.

Individual teachers and particular educational institutions have, as suggested earlier, particular policies or positions with regard to education in general and language teaching in particular. In order to illustrate this briefly and clearly, we can look at one item which always figures largely in any discussion of language: the concept of 'grammar'. Effectively, someone interested in language can define himself or herself quite quickly by seeking to describe this concept. A teacher's view of grammar is crucial to how he or she will teach, and the overall position can be shown, succinctly enough, as follows:

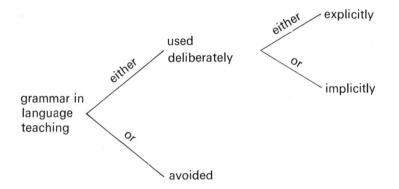

If a teacher uses grammar, then it can either appear openly in the books chosen and the work done (with plenty of rules, exceptions, examples and exercises), or it can be fitted in implicitly, in the organization and gradation of material that superficially appears to be grammar-free. Some teachers, however, regard attempts at using grammar in either of these ways as counter-productive and unnatural, and prefer simply to keep on using language functionally and with no special selection, gradation and presentation until the student acquires it in an unreflecting way. Although this latter idea is attractive to many teachers in principle, most teachers in practical terms belong in the category of grammar-users. They tend to be organized rather than anarchical about rules, and the conservative/radical split is therefore between an explicit as against an implicit use. Such splits or polarities can be shown by means of the following two-column diagram:

	The conservative position	*The radical position*
1	explicit grammar	implicit grammar
2	deductive classroom work	inductive classroom work
3	drills and structures without context	materials organized in both linguistic and situational contexts
4	a prescriptive view of grammar	a descriptive view of grammar
5	an atomistic and analytical approach to language	a holistic and synthetic approach to language
6	a bias towards the graphic medium (reading and writing)	a bias towards the phonic medium (listening and speaking)
7	a diachronic or historical emphasis, particularly relating to literature and 'the classics'	a synchronic or contemporary emphasis, particularly relating to work, holiday interests and culture
8	a preference for teaching formal language styles	a preference for teaching informal language styles
9	an insistence on the value of translation	an insistence on the value of immersion

The conservative position	The radical position
10 emphasis on a homogeneous 'standard' form of a language	emphasis on a heterogeneous and varied use of language
11 a preference for 'chalk and talk' and well-established coursebooks	a liking for audiovisual aids, ways of promoting or provoking interest, and improvising in the classroom
12 a tendency to be suspicious of the science of linguistics	a tendency to be enthusiastic about the science of linguistics, the social sciences, etc., or, at the very least, a willingness to use insights derived from linguistics

A person who is strictly conservative or inclined to be radical has no problem: it is immediately clear where his or her preferences lie. Others, however, may fall into two distinct types:
1 They may have a foot in both camps, preferring to be conservative about some things and radical about others, whether or not they can present well-reasoned accounts of why they have adopted particular positions.
2 They may see no reason to be labelled either way, and may adopt the view that 'it all depends' on circumstances.
A pessimist, faced with the historical development presented in the previous section and the polarities in this section, might shrug and say: 'There's too much to choose from; what a mess!' An optimist, on the other hand, might well look at the fascinating variety of ideas and materials available nowadays and think: 'There's never been so much to choose from, to try, discard, blend, adapt and so on. There's never been a better opportunity to develop a personal, open-minded way of doing things.'

Students, of course, also have their points of view, especially adults, and how the language teacher handles the materials is necessarily linked with how he or she intends to handle the students. An authoritarian with a literary bias and a grammar book at his elbow will lead off in one direction; a free-and-easy libertarian might invite the students to 'share' in the business of learning. The students will agree to go along or not – but one suspects that the thoughtful teacher will look at all the possibilities and be ready for compromise, adaptation, supplementation and the like. There could well be a time for authority and a time for democracy, a time for rules and a time for relaxation, a time for the up-to-the-minute and a time for the long-established. Whatever facilitates the mysterious process of learning is what we are always after: to fit the course to the students and their real needs, rather than to fit the student to an unyielding procrustean bed of a course.

3.9 Being correct and making mistakes

*Attitudes towards the concepts 'correctness' and 'the correction of mistakes'
can be tied in closely with a teacher's general assumptions about the kind of
methods to be used in teaching a language, but – as important matters
relating to the student's motivation – these concepts need to be separately
examined. 'Mistakes' are not so simple a matter as many people suppose.*

The conservatively-inclined teacher has a simple answer as regards what
to teach a student: it is the standard form of the target language, with an
inclination towards formality of style and the literary classics. The spoken
language, when encouraged, will be conceived as needing to avoid as far
as possible such things as 'lazy forms of speech', 'slang expressions' and
'undesirable dialects and accents'. The radically-inclined teacher, on the
other hand, denies that there is any particular virtue in propagating a
middle-class prestige form, and may happily introduce all sorts of informal
'colloquialisms' into his or her classroom work. Such a teacher may not
particularly worry about strict adherence to the rules of grammar, being
much more concerned with the student's efforts to communicate.

Languages are neither rigidly rule-bound nor engines of chaos. They
tend towards patterns of order, and there are large numbers of people who
have strong opinions about what 'good English' or 'le bon français' (etc.)
are. Students are going to meet and talk to such people if and when they
are using their foreign language skills, and in some way they have to be
prepared for these encounters, regardless of the opinions of the teacher
about sociolinguistics. Similarly, students are also going to meet – and need
to understand – all sorts of speech forms which are not formal, literary and
'good', and an enthusiastic student will want to know and use them so as
to avoid the charge of speaking like a book. The teacher has, in some way,
to help lay the foundation for success in this area too. It would seem from
such facts of life that extreme conservative and radical positions are not
the most useful in preparing the student for reality.

Additionally, the teacher's attitude to mistake-making as the student
proceeds with the target language may well have a powerful influence on
motivation, on the wish to continue with the pain and effort as well as the
gratifications of study. If a teacher constantly burdens student and self alike
with red-ink corrections of written work, or the constant stopping and
checking of spoken work, then frustration can reach high levels for all
concerned. The teacher is signalling strongly that the student is a failure,
as opposed to the fact that it takes time and practice to learn a second
language. On the other hand, however, the constant avoidance of criticism
may create a relaxed approach that one can put almost anything together

as long as some sense emerges. Neither of these is particularly useful in real life.

The teacher would seem, therefore, to need some kind of 'even-handed' approach to the making of mistakes, allowing times when a veritable blitz on grammatical faults might be mounted, and times when mistakes are ignored and any achievement on the student's part encouraged – with all sorts of intermediate points. In certain work, the teacher might look to correct only certain kinds of fault, or wait for a pattern of faults to begin to emerge. After all, a student might, with care and the passage of some time, be perfectly capable of correcting his or her own performance. Self-monitoring is a skill worth developing in every student.

The behaviourist view of language learning has urged us to avoid mistakes. The materials should be made mistake-proof, and the students should be steered away from any opportunity to make mistakes. The cognitive view of language learning runs quite the other way, claiming that in the making of mistakes lies the true educational experience of life: students must be free to make mistakes and to put them right in a problem-solving way. As is often the case, there is an element of truth in both these apparently contradictory positions. The student should not be allowed to blunder unnecessarily into mistake-making; nor, however, should the path be made too easy and therefore too dull. Additionally, life doesn't work in an entirely behaviourist or an entirely cognitive way. There *are* times when simple repetitive habit-forming is refreshing and useful, and times when it is deadly dull. There are times when problem-solving is exciting and informative, but there *are* also times when it leads to anger and frustration, because the problem is too hard to solve. Balance here, as elsewhere, seems to be essential, and also, incidentally, allows for variety in the classroom.

Ultimately, however, the question of 'mistakes' comes down to the defining question: what exactly do we mean by a mistake? Mistakes are not all of a kind, as the following list shows:

1 Extending Noam Chomsky's distinction between 'competence' and 'performance', we can talk of 'competence mistakes' on the one hand and 'performance mistakes' on the other. This means that a mistake can arise from a genuine failure to understand and master a systemic element in the target language. The student just does not *know* what to do, does not know for example that the phrase 'bigs houses' is not right in English, whether or not such a construction is the norm in, say, Spanish or French. That kind of thing is a mistake in competence, whereas the kind of mistake that relates to performance is very different indeed: the student knows very well what he or she should have done, but through nervousness, tiredness, pressure, the effects of inner translation (a kind of interference from the home

language) just lapsed and 'forgot' for a moment what to do. A quick and critical teacher, jumping on a performance mistake like this, is more than likely to frustrate the student and reinforce his or her self-disgust. The student is angry about the mistake precisely because it was *not* a competence mistake.

2 It is possible that, in the situation of the foreign learner, performance generally lags behind competence (in pretty much the sense that most students have a greater passive awareness of a language system than an active ability to manipulate it). The students learn, in one way or another, certain usages, understanding them in books and getting them right in formal exercises but are by no means ready to produce flawless performances under pressure. Practice and the chance to feel confident are needed before the intellectually known usages become a performance fact. The student needs time and opportunity to get through the 'mistake barrier' that faces everybody when acquiring a second language. Even then, years after the barrier has been successfully breached smooth performance can be undermined by sudden surprises, emotional upheavals and the like, when even a very competent student will (usually humiliatingly) revert to the pattern of mistakes common to his or her kind of foreign-user in the earlier days of acquiring the second language. The underlying mental and articulatory sets of the home language assert themselves once more.

3 It is odd also that a native-user of a language can get away with all sorts of mistakes that a foreign-user will be penalized for. No one minds very much if a native-user changes grammatical correspondences in mid-sentence, or breaks off and starts again. The foreign-user is, however, often expected – and often bravely expects – to perform perfectly under all circumstances or be judged a failure, something that would not be expected in the mother tongue. At the same time, people expect and sometimes even wait with interest for a competent foreign-user to slip up, whereas we do not normally wait for a native-user to slip up – unless of course we are listening to someone of a different dialect or accent trying for any reason to perform in our dialect or accent. This latter, of course, is common enough among users of prestige dialects, waiting unkindly for the outsider to reveal his or her origin by some kind of 'typical' fault.

Some applied linguists have tried to use the concept of 'error analysis' in a positive way, as a means to help foreign learners towards competence in the target language by analysing the kinds of mistake they are likely to make and then dealing therapeutically with them in advance or as they come up. It has proved surprisingly hard, however, to be both systematic and useful in this area. Charting the typical learner's progress through stages of 'transitional competence' (or various 'interlanguages') is not easy. There is at least one reason why this is so: we are *all* of us transitionally competent (or incompetent) in language, whatever the particular language we are using. An appreciation of this fact – the fundamental difficulty of accurate self-expression – could make all of us gentler in our approach to mistakes and correction.

3.10   Testing language skills

Closely linked with the question of 'mistakes' and 'correction' are the creation and administration of 'tests' and 'examinations'. Such procedures are generally agreed to have a place in foreign-language teaching, and are, like many other areas of interest, subject to controversy. What we think we are doing when we test our students is as revealing about ourselves and our expectations as it is about the abilities of our students.

The simplest way to begin a discussion of testing and evaluation is to propose the following model:

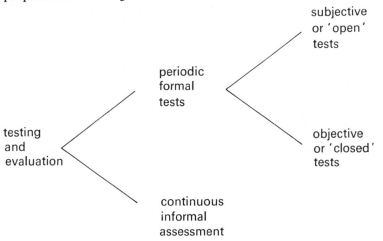

Like the tabulations and lists in the preceding sections, this model outlines various relatively extreme positions in the current argument about testing. A more or less conservative position asserts that formal tests occurring at specific intervals are necessary, for the benefit of both the administration and the student – so that, in effect, we all know where we stand. The radical alternative is antagonistic to this view, asserting that formal tests are psychologically undesirable, creating unnecessary stress in the student and also lacking in real capacity to judge anyone 'objectively'. Such tests should therefore be abandoned, and replaced by the watchful continuous assessment of the student by a presumably always well-disposed and competent tutor or tutors. It is proposed that such tutors know the students best and are in the best of all possible positions to evaluate each individual.

As in all such polarities, it is possible to see good sense on both sides, but not necessarily in the conflict itself. Certainly, tests generate stress, and not only for the students. Teachers, parents and friends and others may become quite powerfully involved in the tensions of exam time, and arguments may arise over the quality and objectivity of the test material and the ability and impartiality of the examiners. It can also be argued, as Desmond Morris does, that institutionalized tests have their origin in the painful puberty rites of pre-technological societies, and that in fact we are engaged in torturing candidates for certain qualifications so that – psychologically – they will appreciate the honour done to them when they pass.

The other side of the coin is not, however, all sweetness and light. Continuous assessment by a friendly and experienced teacher may have much to recommend it – but what about assessment by an unfriendly, less-than-competent teacher, or by someone with a set of grudges to work off? One justification for formal tests has always been that they to a great extent escape from all kinds of partiality – a teacher's over-kindness or wish to see students do well, someone's desire for certain people to shine and others to do badly, and so on. Another quite cogent argument emerges too when we consider that life is not naturally free from stress, and that the initiation rite may to some extent – and subject to changing social conditions – be a psychologically useful way of reminding people that performance under stress is part of being alive in an unpredictable universe.

Many teachers and administrations nowadays have deliberately sought a compromise position between too much reliance on isolated formal tests and too much enthusiasm for continuous friendly assessment. The result is some system of reporting on students that includes both a test-element and an assessment-element from people who know the students' work. Such an 'even-handed' approach seems to take the worst sting out of the tests and the greatest dangers of partiality or enmity out of the personal assessments.

Assuming, however, that some sort of formal testing is either desirable or likely to stay with us for a long time to come, we can look at the second controversy at work in educational circles today. Such a controversy is between those who believe that test items should be free-ranging, both for the setter and the taker of the tests, allowing free expression and even imagination to have their place, and those who seek 'objectivity' as opposed to 'subjectivity' – who want sharp, clear, unambiguous test items that are set and marked according to a strict formula.

The same comments pretty well apply in this controversy as applied with regard to correction and to testing or not testing. Firstly, there is something to be said for allowing a student to perform freely, however hard it may be to give a crisp and clear mark afterwards. There is also something to be said for making sure that both the setter and the taker of the test stay on target – that is, we test and we respond to specific things. When grammatical skills are being tested, we do not let the quality of pronunciation interfere – that kind of thing. Secondly, there is much to be said for short, unambiguous test items that can be marked quickly by a person or, even better, by a machine. 'Yes' and 'no' are easier to assess than any 'well, maybe' answer, however intelligent and interesting such an answer might be. The development of a great deal of sophistication in the making of various multiple-choice or blank-filling tests shows that a good 'objective' test is a valuable tool – but not all objective tests are equally good. The fact that experts on objective testing always stress the need for 'well-constructed test items' that are always 'pre-tested' before finally being given indicates that it is all too easy to make a poor objective test, where either guessing or frustration can upset the testees.

In the arguments between 'objective' and 'subjective' tests one might well hold up for examination the approach adopted by the University of Cambridge Local Examinations Syndicate with regard to the style of tests used in their two certificates for foreign students of English: the First Certificate, and the world-famous Certificate of Proficiency in English. The general procedures adopted since 1975 have sought to balance the objective and subjective approaches to testing, and the new format from 1984 onward continues to refine this policy as follows (listed paper by paper here for the First Certificate):

Paper 1   Reading Comprehension   (1 hour)   OBJECTIVE
Section A: 25 multiple-choice test items
relating to words in sentence contexts, each
item having one correct response and three
distractors
Section B: 15 multiple-choice questions
relating to three or more texts, each item having
one correct response and three distractors

Paper 2   Composition   ($1\frac{1}{2}$ hours)   SUBJECTIVE
two short compositions to be written, out of a
choice of five topics

Paper 3   Use of English   (2 hours)   OBJECTIVE
Section A: a quasi-Cloze procedure test
(filling the blanks in a text), plus various
sentence-manipulation and language-control
exercises
Section B: an exercise in 'directed writing'   SUBJECTIVE
(controlled or guided composition)

Paper 4 Listening Comprehension (c. 30 minutes)   OBJECTIVE
multiple-choice and similar responses to various
recorded passages

Paper 5 Interview (c. 20 minutes)   SUBJECTIVE
Part I: the stimulation of spontaneous
conversation relating to a picture shown to each
candidate individually
Part II: identifying the style and purpose of a
short passage, then reading it aloud (e.g. an
announcement, a set of instructions, the
description of a situation)
Part III: a role-playing exercise relating to a
given situation (e.g. getting information at an
airport)

The examination comprises a total of 5 hours 20 minutes, and of the five papers, two are objective, two are subjective, and one is mixed. Of the time involved, depending on how the candidate divides up the time in Paper 3, about half the overall examination is devoted to each style of testing. In terms of topic sections, there are five subjectively-assessed activities (six, if we count each short essay in Paper 2 separately) as opposed to four objectively-assessed activities, but three of the subjectively-assessed activities last only a few minutes each. All in all – whether for pragmatic or pedagogical reasons, or both – the Examinations Syndicate has temporized elegantly between the two styles, and very probably (as my own experience suggests) to the candidates' advantage. Anyone undergoing five or so hours of this kind of testing, spread over several days, can certainly suppose that his or her English has been examined in terms of listening and speaking, reading and writing. Eclecticism rules, but both conservatives and radicals can claim that their rights have been safeguarded.

There is more to testing, however, than the taking up of methodological positions and the making of satisfactory papers and test items. Testing relates to a multitude of factors which concern both the quality of the teaching given and the learning achieved. In effect, one can test the system as well as the student, and a good test reveals as much about the teachers as about the students. Additionally, testing is not something that stands apart from teaching and learning: teachers are famous for basing their courses on the format of the final examinations ('the backwash effect'), and students and their families are equally famous for treating as irrelevant anything that is not ultimately going to be tested. The trouble here is that, often, we do not teach a subject to our students, but how to pass an exam in that subject.

The positive aspect of this interrelatedness of test and course is that stimulating test material can be woven in with the actual teaching and learning, to the benefit of all concerned. To quote J. B. Heaton:

It is unfortunate that so many examinations in the past have led
to a separation of testing from teaching. Both testing and
teaching are so closely interrelated that it is virtually impossible
to work in either field without being constantly concerned with
the other.
(*Writing English Language Tests*, 1975, p. 1)

Tests, whether small-scale and given in class or large-scale and administered publicly across nations, are all extensions of the teaching and learning situation.

However, tests can vary greatly as regards what examiners may want to know about a candidate, while the same sheet of test items can be used for quite different purposes on different occasions. Thus, while one is always concerned about a test's essential validity, reliability and ability to discriminate among testees, there is also the question of the uses to which it may be put. Such uses can be described quite neatly in terms of the student's position in *time* and the *emphasis* or special interest of the examiner. Most authorities nowadays accept that four main types of test exist. These are, in tabular format:

	Kind of test	*Emphasis or interest on the part of the examiner*
1	the achievement, attainment or progress test	indicating past success or failure in learning and handling material
2	the proficiency test	indicating the level of present ability in a prescribed subject or area
3	the diagnostic test	highlighting current shortcomings (that is, a remedial orientation)
4	the aptitude test	dealing in the future, the candidate's potential in a subject or activity

The *achievement, attainment* or *progress test* is given in order to find out how well a student has done since a certain date, during a certain period of time, probably in a certain kind of formal course. The chances are that the testers know the testees either personally or by repute, and that the testees have all been working according to a common scheme of work. The *proficiency test*, however, is generally more impersonal, and is concerned with the present status of the candidate, quite regardless of past courses or absence of courses. It is what the testees can actually *do* in general terms that matters, not how much better he or she is now than before, or how well a particular dose of material has been assimilated. In all probability, the testers do not know (or even want to know) the testees, or the testees' past history.

The third kind of test is different again. Firstly, the *diagnostic test* is not looking for evidence of capability as such, any more than a doctor is looking for evidence of health in a sick person. The test seeks to classify shortcomings in the testee's abilities, and probably shortcomings that have already been suspected by others involved with the testee. It will in all likelihood serve as the basis for remedial work, so that the testee can then be brought up to some appropriate already-known level or standard. The diagnostic test considers both the past and the present with a view to better performance in the future.

The fourth type of test is entirely free of the past, and little influenced by the present either. The *aptitude test* is concerned with the future possibilities of the testee, and may test him or her in various ways which have little to do with anything learned previously. The testers are looking for signs of a natural ability, and any reasonable way of getting at those signs is acceptable, even if it means testing something that appears to other people as quite irrelevant.

All of these have their place in the language-teaching situation, as does the day-to-day continuing assessment of students by the involved teacher. The great danger in all of them – even the diagnostic test – is that the test becomes more important than the language and the student learning the language. Tests, like many other things, are tools – they are means to ends, and not ends in themselves. Many people can perform very well in foreign languages every day of their lives, yet flunk tests. Many people can perform very well in tests, and yet fail to use the tested language well in the real, on-going test – the outside world.

Ability with languages is all very well in the classroom and the examination hall, but the ultimate test of system, teacher and tester alike is how well the reasonably motivated student does, years later, in the encounters of everyday life, far from home, in the community that uses the target language. Usually, however, nobody reports back on such matters.

3.11 Shaping a language course

The creation of curricula, syllabuses, lesson plans, tests, etc., forms a major part of the organization of language courses within larger educational frameworks. In dealing with such matters, factors to be considered must include not only the immediate methods and materials to be used, but also certain sociolinguistic factors that influence the shape that courses may take. Such factors suggest the need nowadays for a compromise between the demands of the monastery and marketplace traditions.

Language courses, like most other elements in organized education, must have shapes, but just how we approach and realize this idea of shape requires a little thought. The traditional assumption, by and large, has been that the shape of courses devolves from the general shape of both the educational package itself and the institution in which the package is handled; that is, teachers respond to the directives of the ministry of education, the school board, the principal teacher or whatever organization or person decides the general policy of the state and/or the school. In consequence, teachers do not have to do too much thinking: the portions are assigned, they apply what they learned in training college, and the students move through the system.

This traditional process both works and doesn't work. It works, because there is conformity and pressure to conform, there is social momentum and inertia, and departures from the assumed norms are often quite well camouflaged. It doesn't work, because the system at large deals in ideal courses and classes, and every teacher knows that there has never been such a course or class. The ideal and the actual are never isomorphic, and a teacher's problem is often what to do about that fact. The effort to force the actual towards the ideal (or assumed ideal) may often result in complicating everybody's lives so that learning does not proceed as well as it might.

I would propose compromise in this area. Syllabuses are necessary, but they need not be too rigidly specified. When teachers go to their new classes the intended courses can be 'half-planned', with certain things that are clear and must be done, and others that are provisional, depending on how things go. The need to map out every minute dates from the monastery with its bells and its tightly formulated regimen. Today, relevance to everyday life is stressed, and so some compromise has to be made with the give-and-take of the marketplace. Teachers can certainly have their lesson plans and plenty of material in reserve, but flexibility is essential in the struggle to help a group of varied people learn.

Specifically as regards language courses, the norm nowadays seems to be based on the six years of secondary education provided in many countries: six stages in the continuum of a student's adolescent years. Both educational systems and publishers work increasingly on a six-stage plan; the interested reader will find evidence of this not only in the guidelines of ministries but also in the catalogues of such publishers as Longman, Collins and Newbury House, where the following schema operates in one form or another:

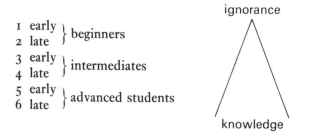

Such an approach is containerization with a vengeance; it has the advantage of structure and gives the impression of security and truth. One knows at least where to pretend to be, despite the heterogeneity of every class that one ever gets, and despite the constant invasion of the classroom by the disorderly world outside. The inverted V of ignorance-to-knowledge beside the six stages suggests here that the student moving through such a course is steadily expanding into the target language, with the implication that, at the end, he or she will be equipped to cope quite well with most of the aspects of the target language in real situations.

This may or may not prove true; what is stage 3 for one part of the world and one kind of learner is certainly not stage 3 for another part of the world and another kind of learner, but in crude general terms the system is workable. It can be made even more workable still if, firstly, we simply accept that it is crude, and, secondly, if we apply some general principles of sociolinguistics to humanize it.

One such principle relates to 'home' language and 'school' language. The standard language used for general purposes in the school is often assumed to be the students' 'mother tongue', but may in fact be a different dialect (very different or only somewhat different). Thus we need to be prepared for the possibility that the school language poses certain social and learning problems, long before we get to a second language. Next, the target offered to the students as a second language resembles, in its country or countries of origin, the school language *there* much more than it resembles many people's everyday language. We can say, succinctly, that a particular school propagates Language A1 while many of its students actually speak A2, and that the foreign-language course offers Language B1, whereas in fact when students go to a country where Language B is used they may encounter B2 or B3 far oftener than they meet B1 (the middle-class standard). Diagrammatically, this may be shown as on p. 117. More speakers of most languages speak 'basilects' than 'acrolects', so that even students who have done well at school will be frustrated in the target foreign country and conclude either that the natives don't speak their own language properly (and are therefore to be disdained), or the school didn't teach the language properly (and is therefore to be condemned in retrospect). George Mikes, in *How to be an Alien*, describes his preference

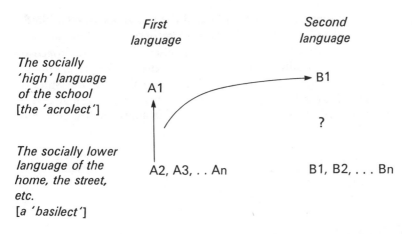

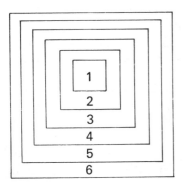

for Budapest English over London English, because he could manage it better. When he went to London for the first time, he had only two problems: he couldn't understand anybody, and nobody could understand him. My wife, after six (successful) years of book English in a Teheran secondary school, had an identical and chastening experience on first arriving in London, and I had a similar experience on first encountering both the French of Provence and of Quebec.

What then can be done? Presumably our attitude towards the school-year containers should be modified. We can agree that they cannot be jettisoned completely, for after all some structure is needed, and certainly in the early years standardization, selection, grading, etc., are all essential. However, we may agree that we teach rules in order to move beyond them, that we use boxes in order to escape from them. In consequence, the first and innermost box can remain what it always was: small, secure, womb-like, safe; but as we move through the years the students should be exposed to more and more variety in the target language – more accents, more styles, more people, more situations (simulated or real), more visits (if possible). The narrower and less helpful view of things might look like this:

Here, we are governed by the limitations of the coursebooks, etc., blindly followed as good and sufficient. What I am proposing (and what many successful teachers already do, explicitly or implicitly), is a more broken-up approach, one that gradually allows more of the marketplace into the monastery (in manageable doses for all concerned), until the students become aware of what language reality is, and can go on to their careers and their trips abroad more confidently. For this approach, the model is:

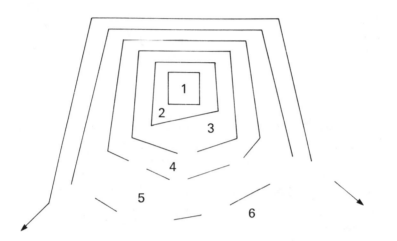

The model as I have drawn it here is still a structured entity, opening up to the world in only one direction. Nonetheless, it is wide open when compared with the tight monastery style of the preceding model. It could be wider open still, with the walls breaking down not just in one or two but in three or four directions. In all such cases, however, there would be a safe 'core', the starting place that has its walls intact and provides a firm base for future activity. Within such a model, we can respect what is useful in both the more traditional and the more modern approaches to language teaching and learning, helping our students take risks and then return to the security of what they already know well. In the process they would meet up with all the problems of standard and dialect, formality and slang, while still being equipped with clear guidelines; and in the process, we might even generate a little more linguistic toleration than is at present detectable in the world.

A model of this kind implicitly asserts that courses will vary according to time, place, students and students' needs (leaving aside for the moment the personality, interests and aptitudes of the teacher). It provides for growth and experimentation as well as the probability that no two courses will ever be the same. One might indeed even be surprised or disturbed if two courses *were* pretty much the same. Given the range of materials available to us today, and a generation of teachers able to create further materials from the world around them, this kind of model allows us, for the first time on a mass scale, the opportunity to organize tailor-made or custom-built courses for groups and even individuals. Chef-like, we can take some X, add a unit of Y, lightly sprinkle with Z, and come up with a concoction that is both efficient and humane. *That* is an intriguing prospect.

Appendix 1 Using *A Foundation Course for Language Teachers* in teacher-training courses

There is no single valid way in which this book can be used in any one course or group of courses; the tutor's aims, needs and special emphases, as well as the nature of the institution's programme, will inevitably decide the most practical approach to it in particular circumstances.

Part 1: Linguists and language can go readily in any of several kinds of basic course for teacher-trainees simply as a means of alerting them to the nature of language, or can go in or with a specific course relating linguistics to language teaching. *Part 2: Twenty-five centuries of grammar* can also go into one or more background courses, or into a course specifically linked with the study and use of grammar as a concept and as an educational tool. *Part 3: The gift of tongues?* can go in any course on general methodology, either as a contribution to theory, or as complementary reading for those engaged in teaching practice or the reviewing of methods and materials. *A Foundation Course for Language Teachers* can be a main element in a course or an element drawn into a course as and when necessary. It can be a coursebook which everyone possesses, a group tool, or a shelf reference book, according to need. I developed and used the material in its current form for basic first-degree courses in language-teaching methodology and the teaching of English as a second language. I have also used various elements in courses on the English language, on applications of phonetics, on the use of audio-visual aids and teaching materials, and so forth. Additionally, I have adapted the various parts for use in in-service training programmes and summer institutes for practising teachers.

A book like this can be used in a course in any of at least five ways:

1 It can be read by the students outside classroom time, usually in doses allocated for certain times when the class will meet and its content can be discussed.

2 The tutor can discuss aspects of the material in class (through lectures, tutorials, group work, with or without brief handouts), then assign follow-up reading outside the classroom.

3 The tutor can read aloud excerpts from the book (or provide these excerpts separately) as a basis for further personal comment and/or the stimulation of class discussion, with or without insisting on structured reading assignments outside the class.

4 The tutor can read the book aloud section by section personally or get the students to do the reading in turns until the material is covered, after which some kind of formal examination might be held.

5 The tutor can use a judicious combination of 1 to 4.

My personal preference is a combination of techniques 1 and 2, and an occasional use of 3. Technique 4 has never appealed to me much; for me it is an uninspiring use of limited and valuable contact time with the students. Short direct lectures and talks (that ride the rhythm of the students' attention spans) are useful, as long as students know they can at certain points come in with questions that will get a decent answer, or with other contributions, the whole leading towards guided discussion. In such discussion, one's own questions should serve to elicit what *ought* to be said as well as observations that one could never possibly have anticipated (and that often have enormous value for the course). Additionally, I have always tended to pepper teaching sessions with stories of various kinds, jokes, analogies and queries about the students' lives and attitudes that can apparently move things away from the subject but then come swinging back in again. A little drama of this kind does no harm, and often works wonders for the concentration.

Supplementary and complementary source material should also be readily available for the students to consult, so that they can expand their understanding of what is happening out into the work of other writers and into a link-up with other information. A course like this should not be incestuous. It is also good when a student can bring in a source discovered elsewhere that one may have overlooked or never knew; such a find can be brought to the attention of the others publicly, and suitably acknowledged.

Requirements for evaluation and final grades, etc., vary, but can generally be met by a suitable combination of the following:

1 a continuing assessment of a student's general participation in the work of the class. This might include, for example, service as a group leader who has to sum up the group's work, participation in a small project defining a term like 'grammar' or searching for specific answers to questions. It could also relate to the student's constructiveness in general discussions.

2 a term paper for which an initial proposal is submitted and approved. The student could choose a subject from among a list such as is available here in appendix 3, or set out on something of genuine personal interest. Such a paper should be a serious piece of work using the basic paraphernalia of scholarship in a consistent and thorough way.

3 a mid-term test (preferably linked to review questions such as in appendix 2, which the students will be aware of in advance).

4 an end-of-session examination with review elements and some opportunity for the student to demonstrate an ability to think independently. Such a test could contain set questions (multiple-choice, true-or-false, fill-in, etc.) as one component, and open-ended material inviting personal responses as the other, much as I recommend in section 3.10.

5 a five-minute lecturette on an aspect of the course, the topic approved in advance of presentation.

These are options, and they can vary from course to course. It is undesirable, however, for the students to feel constantly under evaluative surveillance. They should be able to forget the tutor's role as judge for at least half of the time they are engaged on the work of the course.

Feedback is vital, whether it proves complimentary or otherwise. The students should leave the course feeling stretched, intrigued and informed – even provoked into *not* thinking of the coursework as over and done with, but as something for them to make part of their professional lives. The tutor should have some knowledge of what has been going on in their minds; short and simple questionnaires are probably still the best ways of getting them to record their comments, but talking to them at break or on other occasions is just as valuable. Written comments can be filed and courses adapted where the feedback indicates that something ought to be done. The negative comments are at least as valuable as the positive, if not sometimes more valuable, and quite often comments come through that make it all worthwhile several times over. Here are some comments from my own students:

- 'The graphic message on linguistics has developed deep interest in the science, and more specifically in its human aspects, i.e. communication and understanding.' (Hélene Quesnel)
- 'The first time I tried to read the material I fell asleep after ten minutes, from general exhaustion!...The handbook stimulated an appetite for more, however, particularly on our failure to communicate well.' (Louisette Pouliot)
- 'The reading of the handbook provides a common ground for the discussion of language; we all now know more or less what we're talking and thinking about.' (France Jutras)
- 'These principles are accepted by most linguists. Wouldn't it be great if they were also accepted by most societies?' (Barry Gallant)
- 'The main purpose of the handbook was to demystify the phenomenon of language...Linguistics, I now believe, can be important if not fundamental to all future (language) teachers.' (Jocelyne Chalifoux)
- 'Language is more complex than I thought.' (Louis Toussignant)
- 'My perspective on linguistics has changed from being somewhat myopic to a more searching attitude.' (Ginette Hamel)
- 'My response...is an emotional one. Suddenly, I had before me, set out in a logical, rational way, the expression of very deep, but disjointed, feelings that I have had for years.' (Mary Glen Cownie)
- 'I find the images of a "monastic tradition" and a "marketplace tradition" in the acquiring of a language picturesque and evocative' – 'As I read about grammar I felt, metaphorically speaking,

as if I were in a plane flying over 2,500 years of the history of the mind.' (Aglaja Schnitter)

- 'I must admit that my reaction altered over time. My initial impressions were that the author had taken what I thought was a simple concept, language, and flogged it to death...However, as I continued reading, and began reflecting on the thoughts expressed, I realized that my first reaction...originated from my absolute absence of introspective study in the area of language; I had taken it for granted.' (Herbert McFaull)
- 'I greatly appreciated reading the material on grammar. Not having studied the classical languages I have for the first time become aware of the great amount of work that the ancient grammarians accomplished.' (Jocelyne Tellier)
- 'After having read this, I realize how very little I actually knew about grammar. Having been a child of the sixties, I have never come in contact with formal instruction of grammar, or at least not until I studied translation. Its history seems to reflect the history of many other domains. The past directly influences the present or even repeats itself under a different name.' (Elizabeth-Anne Malischewski)

It is always, ultimately, the students who define a course.

Appendix 2 Basic review questions

The following lists of questions are intended for revision purposes. They can be used to refresh the mind as to the central issues in the book, for individuals to check their personal success in remembering salient points, for classroom review work, and as the basis of formal and informal tests. The sections where the answers to the questions can be found are given in brackets after each question.

Part 1: Linguists and language

1   How has the scientific method been applied over the last five centuries? (1.0)
2   In what sense can we be said to have taken language for granted? (1.0)
3   What two comments are made about language in the quotation from de Saussure? (1.0)
4   What makes language difficult to study scientifically? (1.0)
5   What does it mean when we say that linguistics is not dependent on a traditional mythology? (1.1)
6   What is the difference between 'objective' and 'descriptive', and 'subjective' and 'prescriptive'? (1.1)
7   What is meant by saying that linguistics is relativistic? (1.1)
8   What is to be understood by the statement that linguistics is autonomous? (1.1)
9   Why is it necessary to point out that linguistics is concerned with *all* aspects of language? (1.1)
10   In what sense can some animal species be said to have language? (1.2)
11   In what sense must we, on the basis of present knowledge, exclude animals from having language? (1.2)
12   What remarkable factors form part of the effort a child makes when learning its first language? (1.3)
13   What two historical traditions must be borne in mind when considering the development of language-teaching methods? (1.4)
14   In what way can they be said to be in conflict today? (1.4)
15   How can a language be both a system of arbitrary conventions and yet invested with a great deal of emotional loyalty? (1.5)

16   What is the Sapir–Whorf Hypothesis? (1.6)
17   What are its 'strong' and 'weak' aspects? (1.6)
18   In what sense can language be said to have a dual organization? (1.7)
19   Why is it important to distinguish between the various mediums? (1.8)
20   What is an articulatory set? (1.9)
21   What is body language? (1.9)
22   What are personal space and social distance? (1.9)
23   In what way is interpenetration inescapable among languages? (1.10)
24   In what way can it be said that all languages have equal potential? (1.11)
25   Why do linguists say that no language is static? (1.12)
26   Why do linguists say that no language is homogeneous? (1.13)
27   What do the terms 'synchronic' and 'diachronic' mean? (1.12)
28   What is an idiolect? (1.4 and 1.13)
29   What is a dialect? (1.13)
30   What is a standard? (1.13)
31   What do people do in free situations where they badly need to communicate somehow across languages? (1.14)
32   What happens in Area C when Languages A and B meet there? (1.14)
33   In what sense is it sometimes hard to decide whether a community's speech form is a language or a dialect? (1.14)
34   What is a model? (1.15)
35   What can be said about grammar and models of language? (1.15)
36   What simple models of language are shown in section 1.15?
37   In what sense can we say that languages are both conservative and innovative at the same time? (1.16)
38   What is sociolinguistics? (1.16)
39   What is psycholinguistics? (1.17)
40   What is neurolinguistics? (1.17)
41   From what does language ultimately derive? (1.17)
42   What can be said about comparing the brain and a computer? (1.17)
43   What is context and what are its various aspects? (1.18)
44   What is a co-text? (1.18)
45   Why is context so important for people working with language? (1.18)
46   What two kinds of competence have linguists been interested in? (1.19)
47   What, approximately, is the relationship between grammar (etc.), philology and linguistics? (1.20)

48 What main points can be made about European linguistics? (1.20)
49 What main points can be made about British linguistics? (1.20)
50 What main points can be made about linguistics in the United States? (1.20)

Part 2: Twenty-five centuries of grammar

51 Why is 'grammar' difficult? (2.0)
52 What does Dinneen assert about the terminology of traditional grammar? (2.0)
53 Why is grammar generally not a popular subject? (2.0)
54 What evidence is there of a possible renaissance of interest in grammar? (2.0)
55 Why have I compared the 'long-gone breakthrough' of the invention of writing to the modern computer revolution? (2.1)
56 Why have I felt the need for a term like 'orature'? (2.1)
57 With what other subjects was the study of grammar linked in ancient Greece? (2.1)
58 What is the origin in Greek of the term 'grammar'? (2.2)
59 Why was grammar popularly linked with sorcery in the Middle Ages? (2.2)
60 What was the point of the ancient controversy about nature and convention? (2.3)
61 What was the point of the subsequent controversy about analogy and anomaly? (2.3)
62 What present-day grammatical and language-teaching concept emerged from the analogy–anomaly controversy? (2.3)
63 How does the process of analogy work? (2.3)
64 Which two grammarians of the ancient world most shaped traditional grammar? (2.3)
65 What were the three basic parts of speech in ancient Greece? (2.4)
66 What two ancient Greek constructs lie behind the modern sentence? (2.5)
67 Why does Dinneen suggest that traditional grammarians may still be 'translating languages into Greek, even though they may know no Greek'? (2.5)
68 What did the modern linguist Leonard Bloomfield try to do in his approach to grammar? (2.5)
69 What is a paradigm? (2.6)
70 What metaphor did the ancient Greeks use to describe variations in the grammatical forms of nouns? (2.6)
71 What does the word 'conjugation' mean, in etymological terms? (2.7)

72 Were the grammarians of ancient Rome determined to make Latin fit into a Greek grammatical mould? (2.6 and 2.7)

73 What was the status of the Latin language in the Middle Ages? (2.7)

74 By what term were the newer European languages known? (2.7)

75 What was the general view of medieval scholars about the newer European languages and Latin? (2.7)

76 For which part of speech in many European languages is the Latin paradigm still useful? (2.7)

77 What is Palmer's basic assertion about the effect of the study of Latin grammar on the study of English grammar? (2.7)

78 What is morphology? (2.8)

79 What kind of problems do we face when we seek to distinguish morphology from syntax? (2.8)

80 What suggestion did Jespersen make about a somewhat different approach to morphology and syntax? (2.8)

81 What is the chain–choice relationship? (2.9)

82 What are the technical terms used by linguists today for this relationship? (2.9)

83 What common modern teaching device is based on the chain–choice relationship? (2.9)

84 What is distribution? (2.9)

85 Under what circumstances does the idea of the grammarian as legislator arise? (2.10)

86 Why might it be said that users of English have different attitudes about grammar from users of, say, French and Italian? (2.10)

87 Why have educational systems developed since the end of the eighteenth century tended to use grammar as an educational tool? (2.10)

88 What events and activities led in the nineteenth century to tension between prescriptive and descriptive approaches to grammar? (2.10)

89 In what way has politics entered into this area of tension? (2.10)

90 What new usage has developed in relation to the term 'grammar' with the growth of linguistic science?

91 In what way do pedagogical grammars differ from theoretical grammars even though they may be derived from them? (2.10)

92 What element in human nature does the study of grammar derive from? (2.11)

93 What is 'natural internal grammar'? (2.11)

94 In what sense is all language artificial? (2.11)

95 What are the characteristics of primary grammar? (2.11)

96 What are the characteristics of secondary grammar? (2.11)

97 What are the two aspects of secondary grammar? (2.11)

98　Why does one's attitude to the concept 'rule' differ according to one's view of grammar? (2.11)

99　What two reasons might a person have for saying someone has 'bad grammar'? (2.11)

100 What is the main difference between prescriptive and descriptive grammar, according to point 11? (2.11)

Part 3: The gift of tongues?

101 Why can the teaching of languages nowadays be called an industry? (3.0)

102 Why should we try to reconcile what I call here the macrocosm and microcosm? (3.0)

103 What accidents of birth and circumstances are so obvious that we often forget that they *are* just accidents? (3.1)

104 What sort of reasons do language enthusiasts often give for learning foreign languages? (3.1)

105 What actual reasons may people have for learning foreign languages? (3.1)

106 What pressures operate at times to reduce people's willingness to learn foreign languages? (3.1)

107 What are teacher-proof materials? (3.2)

108 Is there any justification for them? (3.2)

109 What general matters make up what I call the sociocultural matrix from which teaching cannot be separated? (3.2)

110 What everyday physical factors can affect the success or failure of classroom work? (3.2)

111 What everyday human and social factors can affect the success or failure of classroom work? (3.2)

112 Why are self-motivation and self-discipline important factors in the professionalism of the teacher? (3.2)

113 What is the relationship between enthusiasm for and knowledge of one's subject? (3.2)

114 What points are worth noting about a sound knowledge of one's subject? (3.2)

115 What is a person's attention span and what should a teacher seek to do about it? (3.2)

116 What ways are available to us as means of considering the teacher–student–materials relationship? (3.3)

117 Why are a teacher's worldview and general philosophy of life significant factors in teaching? (3.4)

118 What are the extreme positions between which a teacher's conception of his or her work can move? (3.4)

119 The teaching of first and second languages is not the same, but what six factors are worth considering as evidence of certain fundamental similarities? (3.5)

120 What is code-switching? (3.5)

121 What factors characterize the tradition of formal language instruction passed on to us by the Greeks and Romans? (3.6)

122 What is the name generally given nowadays to this tradition? (3.6)

123 What characterizes the 'marketplace' way of learning languages? (3.6)

124 What characterizes the 'monastery' way of learning languages? (3.6)

125 What forces have helped to create present-day school organizations, aims and tensions? (3.6)

126 Was the grammar–translation method an educational monolith in by-gone centuries? (3.7)

127 What characterized the revolution in language teaching in the late nineteenth century? (3.7)

128 What is a 'method', and what are the temptations inherent in thinking in terms of 'methods'? (3.7)

129 How does an 'approach' differ from a 'method'? (3.7)

130 What is the bandwagon effect? (3.7)

131 What main points are made about the grammar–translation method in the review of methods and approaches? (3.7)

132 What main points are made about the direct method, etc., in the same review? (3.7)

133 What main points are made about structural approaches and structuralism in the review? (3.7)

134 What main points are made about situationalism? (3.7)

135 What main points are made about the communicative approach and notional–functionalism? (3.7)

136 Do we at present have a scientifically respectable and comprehensive theory of language learning on which to base our teaching work? (3.7)

137 What overall schematic description is offered for language teachers' general responses to the teaching of grammar? (3.8)

138 How do I characterize the differences between the conservative and radical positions in language teaching? (3.8)

139 What conclusions can be drawn from the distinctive preferences of the two extreme kinds of language teacher (and what solution do I suggest)? (3.8)

140 What are the likely effects of a policy of constantly correcting students' work? (3.9)

141 What are the likely consequences of a laissez-faire policy towards students' errors? (3.9)

142 What approach is advised in the text? (3.9)

143 What is the behaviourist view of mistake-making? (3.9)

144 What is the cognitive view of mistake-making? (3.9)

145 What two kinds of mistake-making emerge from the discussion of a student's knowledge of the system of a language? (3.9)

146 What is the aim of error analysis? (3.9)

147 What overall schematic description is offered for teachers' general responses to the idea of testing and evaluation? (3.10)

148 What are the arguments for and against periodic formal tests? (3.10)

149 What are the arguments for and against continuous assessment? (3.10)

150 What are the arguments for and against 'subjective' tests? (3.10)

151 What are the arguments for and against 'objective' tests? (3.10)

152 What solutions do I suggest, and what example do I offer as regards the subjective–objective problem? (3.10)

153 What are the four main types of test? (3.10)

154 What is the traditional approach to the organization of courses? (3.11)

155 What can be said about the effectiveness of the traditional approach? (3.11)

156 What is the prevailing way of dividing up the stages in formal foreign-language learning in secondary schools, etc.? (3.11)

157 What has to be recalled about the nature of the first and second languages in which the teacher and student are working in order to create a course that may hope to be successful in practical terms? (3.11)

158 What are basilects and acrolects? (3.11)

159 What problem does the example from George Mikes emphasize? (3.11)

160 What solution have I offered here to the problems described and how is it represented schematically? (3.11)

Appendix 3   Topics for project work

The following topics, organized according to the parts and sections of the book to which they directly relate, can serve as the basis for a variety of projects: private reflection, group discussion, reports or essays, detailed term papers, group research projects, and so on. There is far more material here than will normally be needed in a term or semester, and selections can be made from among the various items according to need.

Part 1: Linguists and language

SECTION 1.0

1   Language as a social tool
2   You are a lexicographer and must define the word 'language' for a new dictionary. Rough out a basic definition, then consider it in relation to the definitions in several standard dictionaries (Webster, Oxford, Longman, Chambers, Random House, etc.). If you belong to a group, the various members can compare results and consider the stages through which their thinking developed. One member of the group might draw up a report on the whole experiment and keep it for reconsideration at the end of the course.

SECTION 1.1

3   The distinguishing features of modern linguistic science
4   'Linguistics is concerned with *all* aspects of language equally.' Is this, in your view, a realistic claim or goal?

SECTION 1.2

5   Animal 'languages'
6   Are human beings animals? In discussing this question, examine not only your intellectual but also your emotional response to the idea.

SECTION 1.3

7   Discuss my assertion that child language acquisition can be considered 'a recurring human miracle'. Is it in your view a reasonable observation or an exaggeration?
8   The nature–nurture controversy

SECTION 1.4

9 Factors influencing foreign or second language learning in...
(Choose a part of the world that you know or that interests you.)
10 Discuss the idea of the monastery and marketplace traditions in
relation to your own educational experience and to any other
systems of education or societies that you know or that interest
you. Is this idea a useful and accurate one, in your view?

SECTION 1.5

11 Arbitrariness and emotion in our use of language
12 Discuss Schrödinger's observations in relation to your own
experiences using the languages you know. One of my students, a
native-user of French, once described her English in a moment of
frustration as 'like handling a rose with boxing gloves'. Can you
identify with that statement as regards your second or third
language?

SECTION 1.6

13 The Sapir–Whorf Hypothesis
14 Using the observations of Lyons and Tyler as a base, consider
further the problems that arise in translating from one language to
another or one cultural position to another. You can refer both to
general principles and personal experience.

SECTION 1.7

15 Duality of organization in language: medium and message
16 How do you respond to the idea of telepathy? Linguistics and
science at large have expressed little direct interest in it. Do you
consider it a possibility, a fact, or a delusion? What would life be
like if we were telepaths as opposed to or in addition to being
language-users?

SECTION 1.8

17 Actual and possible language mediums (You may wish to introduce
into this review a discussion of communication and such handicaps
as deafness and blindness.)
18 Discuss the differences between speech and writing as mediums of
language. Can factors which are important in one be used in
discussing the other (that is, can the way a word is spelled be used
as a factor in discussing its pronunciation)?

SECTION 1.9

19 Body language
20 What differences have you personally noticed or been told about in the body language, personal space and other cultural conventions of communities that you know or are interested in? Can they cause misunderstandings among people of different backgrounds? Your group (if any) may have a number of stories related to this area of language and cultural interest.

SECTION 1.10

21 Languages in contact
22 How do you respond personally to the idea that language purity is something of an illusion? Is there any sense in which insisting upon 'standards' is important? Can anyone legislate to stop one language influencing another?

SECTION 1.11

23 Languages: potentially equal but actually diverse
24 Discuss the ways in which languages borrow from each other – English from French, French from English, English from Italian for musical terms, and so on. What special examples of this permanent interaction of languages do you know, and how do you feel about them?

SECTION 1.12

25 The axes of diachrony and synchrony
26 Consider the changes through time that have occurred in the languages you know, especially, say, between older people still alive and adolescents. In this respect, you can look at slang, catchwords, special interest areas like computers and video games, sports, and so on. Have newspaper styles changed much since, say, 1900? Have attitudes to formality and modes of address, older and younger people, women and men, social groups, etc., changed, and has language changed accordingly?

SECTION 1.13

27 Diversity in language
28 Have differences in idiolect, accent and dialect affected your life in any way, or the lives of people known to you? In discussing this area of interest, you can consider, say, differences between language styles in a capital city and remoter country areas, attitudes to

people who acquire 'refined' accents, persons with speech defects such as a cleft palate or stammering, children's attitudes to newcomers in their school with 'funny accents', and other comparable matters.

SECTION 1.14

29　Language, society and politics
30　You may be aware of some special area of language contact or conflict that has become part of the life of a particular place (like French and English in Quebec, Spanish and English among Puerto Ricans; or relationships among official, national, regional, tribal, vernacular and other languages in many parts of the world). Discuss your personal experience of such contacts and conflicts and consider them in relation to linguistics, education and language teaching.

SECTION 1.15

31　Making, judging and using models of language
32　Can language be discussed at all without making some kind of model, however rough-and-ready, in order to serve as a basis for that discussion?

SECTION 1.16

33　Language in society
34　Discuss any or all of the following in relation to a language or languages you know and use:
　　(a) formal and informal modes, as for example in addressing people, in using pronouns and in reference to people of different kinds
　　(b) colloquial and literary styles: what could go in a book but not in everyday conversation, and vice versa
　　(c) strong language: taboos and euphemisms when people swear or need to express themselves forcefully or tactfully

SECTION 1.17

35　Try to define the terms 'mind', 'brain' and 'thought'. Consider how you feel while doing this, and how you feel when you stop.
36　Discuss the possibility that one day computer-like machines will use human language. How do you feel about this? What will the machines need to be able to do in order to be successful users of language? Do you think such a thing likely or unlikely, and if likely how soon?

SECTION 1.18

37 Language in and out of context
38 Try to create a set of sentences exhibiting contextual problems in relation to just one word, as I have done with the item *man*.
39 Discuss a few synonyms in any language you know and consider the ways in which they are used and the degree to which they can in fact be called synonyms. (Some examples in English are 'man', 'fellow' and 'guy', or 'big', 'large' and 'great'.)

SECTION 1.19

40 The concept of competence in language
41 What is important in successful communication? How many factors can you list that are significant? Which of these factors are immediate and crucial, which simply desirable? What social and environmental conditions can affect one's fluency and success? What personal factors can affect them? Do you consider success in communication an actuality, or an ideal towards which we aim, or should aim?

SECTION 1.20

42 A short history of language study
43 How do you feel about language and linguistics now that you have completed your reading and coursework for this part of the book? How do you feel about the relevance of linguistics to the profession of language teaching? Do you feel inclined or disinclined to increase your knowledge of linguistics?

Part 2: Twenty-five centuries of grammar

SECTION 2.0

44 What is your own intellectual and emotional response to the word 'grammar'?
45 Consider what I have done with the words 'fire' and 'grammar', then try to create a similar set of sentences to demonstrate the polysemic nature of a word.

SECTION 2.1

46 The origins of writing
47 How do you react to the fact that in ancient India mathematical treatises were written in verse? What is the value of poetry to you?

Is your feeling about traditional poetry similar to your feeling about traditional grammar, or quite different? If you are in a group, discuss these points and try to draw some general conclusions.

SECTION 2.2

48 Grammar and glamour: how words and concepts change
49 Consider why popular and informed responses to such things as writing, grammar, yoga, chemistry and computers can be so different. Why are the popular responses to such things so often tinged with awe, suspicion and even fear?

SECTION 2.3

50 The inventors of grammar
51 Discuss the use of analogical reasoning in learning to use a language, and the problems that children and foreign learners sometimes have because of the incompleteness of analogical systems. (You might also like to try extending certain analogies so that they no longer work properly or become ridiculous, as I did with *mouse: mice:: house: hice*.)

SECTION 2.4

52 The birth of the sentence and the part it plays in our civilization
53 Make up a list of about ten or twelve sentences that have about fifteen words each, or take them from a newspaper or other source. If you are in a group, test the members on the speed and accuracy with which they can identify *all* the parts of speech in every sentence. Discuss the results.

SECTION 2.5

54 In reading this material so far, if you are anything like my students, you have been either:
    (a) sorry, angry or perturbed because you have little or no knowledge of Latin and Greek and therefore feel at a kind of disadvantage, or
    (b) you are relieved that you have had enough of a traditional classical education to feel at home with the terms and ideas used here.
    If you have either of these responses, is either of them valid?
55 (a) Grammar is dull, always has been dull, always will be dull: nothing will change this fact.

(b) Grammar is interesting because it is at the heart of communication.

(c) Well, it isn't as dull as I thought it would be.

Which of these statements comes nearest to your present general response to grammar? Discuss your response in relation to the material so far in part 2.

SECTION 2.6

56 Should Latin be offered nowadays as a school or college course? What arguments can be mustered for and against the teaching of a classical language?

57 You may belong to a culture which has a classical language or language form comparable to Latin. Consider its place in your culture generally and in your own life.

SECTION 2.7

58 How do you feel about teaching and learning languages by means of paradigms and similar devices?

59 How do you respond to the 'debate' that I have conducted with Palmer? A colleague has suggested to me that I am in fact trying here to reinstate the grammar–translation method as a viable means of teaching languages. Is this in your opinion what I am doing?

SECTION 2.8

60 Which do you prefer: the traditional view of morphology and syntax, or Jespersen's – or do you find the whole discussion arid?

61 Discuss either or both of my points about 'teapot' and 'is jumping'? How would you explain these things to an interested learner of English?

SECTION 2.9

62 Experiment with various shorter and longer sentences until you can set up chain–choice relationships easily, following my style with *The cat sat on the mat*. Box the results and turn them into substitution tables (where possible). Such constructs serve as devices for the sentence pattern practice that structuralist teachers of language enjoy using. What do you think about them?

63 'Paradigmatic and syntagmatic relations could be the basic building system of language.' Discuss.

SECTION 2.10

64 The grammarian: legislator or observer?
65 Should a prestigious insitution have as one of its aims the proper instruction of the public in how to use a national language correctly?
66 Is the development and strengthening of national standard languages a plot on the part of the bourgeoisie against the working class?

SECTION 2.11

67 Can primary and secondary grammar be kept apart in the mind of an educated person? If people have primary grammar as the gift of their community while growing up, do they in fact have any need for secondary grammar?
68 Now that you have completed the work of the course, what is your general response to its content? Has your attitude towards the concept 'grammar' altered in any significant way, positively or negatively?

Part 3: The gift of tongues?

SECTION 3.0

69 Language teaching: a service industry?
70 Why do you (or did you) want to become a language teacher? As a language teacher, do you feel that it is necessary to be aware of vast historical processes at work in the world, or do you wish that people and the world would just leave you alone to get to know your students and get on with the job?

SECTION 3.1

71 Consider yourself as honestly as possible. Do you have a deep inner certainty that your mother tongue is the best language on earth, providing the clearest vision of how reality is, or do you genuinely see it as something you acquired simply by 'an accident of sociobiology'?
72 Check where you are in the categories describing why people learn or don't learn certain languages. You can do this on your own or in a group, and keep tally with boxes like the following:

Why people learn certain languages

1 through government decision	2 for career reasons	3 from family interest	4 because of special links with the language	5 for the sake of it

Why people don't learn certain languages

1 a uni-lingual society	2 influence of the home language	3 badly taught mother tongue	4 badly taught second language	5 social and political pressures	6 personal factors

SECTION 3.2

73 How do you respond to the idea of 'teacher-proof materials'? Is it a necessary and practical idea, or is it an insult?

74 I talk in this section of the influence upon classwork of 'the endless soap opera of school, college and university'. Is this to be taken as a fair or even a serious comment?

75 Discuss the idea of professionalism. Consider the reasons why people accept medicine and the law as clearcut professions, and then relate these criteria to teaching in general and language teaching in particular. What are your conclusions?

76 Is a person's attention span important, and do teachers that you know and have known (including yourself) give conscious attention to it, or at least perform as though it signified?

SECTION 3.3

77 Discuss the teacher–student–materials relationship in terms of your own experience as both student and teacher or teacher-trainee. What are you own inclinations, explicit or implicit, in this matter? What are your colleagues' or fellow students' inclinations?

78 Examine any of the following:
the teacher as revered guide
surrogate father or mother
policeman or child-minder
actor
resource person
the friend who knows

persecutor
victim
or any other image-cum-role that interests you.

79 Examine any of the following:
the student as sitting at the feet of the master
empty jar to be filled
eternal child
prisoner
audience
consumer
the friend who doesn't know
persecutor
victim
or any other image-cum-role that interests you.

SECTION 3.4

80 Is there any real need, in your view, to go so far into the personal concerns and private lives of teachers? Does it matter what personal ideologies and attitudes a teacher may have? And if it does or does not matter, what then? What does one do about religious disagreements, political conflicts and witch-hunts, personal vendettas for ideological reasons, and so on?

81 Consider yourself as honestly as possible. What taboos (like never drinking alcohol or coffee, or eating meat), what preferences or obsessions (like golf or video games or the legalizing of pot or the preservation of whales), what likes and dislikes (regarding food, clothes, cosmetics, smoking, hygiene, and so on), what biases (like feminism or a political position), etc., do you have that might make you behave in your place of work in a significantly different way from the norm? What consequences (if any) might such factors have?

82 Where would you put yourself or any other teacher you know on the continuum below?

×—————————————————————————×
teacher as   teacher as
socializer   instructor
or social   or pedagogue
worker

SECTION 3.5

83 Teaching first and second languages: the similarities and the differences

84 Which of the six points that I make about the similarities in teaching the home and target languages have a special significance for you?

SECTION 3.6

85 Monks or merchants: which do language teachers resemble more?
86 What, in your opinion and speaking as both a language enthusiast and a realist, is the value of a second language in the modern world?
87 If and when we succeed in teaching a language well to one or more students (or at least if that student or those students succeed in learning it well in our company), has that success occurred *despite* the system or because of it? Or is life too complex a matter for us to make such simple statements?

SECTION 3.7

88 Using whatever other sources you need or can find, develop my account of the history of language-teaching material into a full essay.
89 Choose any one leading method or approach, consult whatever other sources are available to you (including actual teaching materials), consider the strengths and weaknesses of that method or approach, and write a detailed report.
90 Write a detailed report on either language-teaching technology or visual aids or both, drawing upon whatever other sources are available to you.

SECTION 3.8

91 Discuss the implications of my comments on teachers and the teaching of grammar in relation to any elements that appear in *Part 2: Twenty-five centuries of grammar* that seem to you to be relevant.
92 Convert my tabular representation of the positions of the conservative and the radical into a continuous survey, adding additional material of your own wherever necessary.

SECTION 3.9

93 What is your personal view of correction and mistake-making? What experience have you had of various teachers' policies in these areas, and what do you yourself do or plan to do?
94 Going to whatever sources are available to you for further information, discuss the impact of behaviourism and cognitive psychology as two conflicting psychological theories upon language teaching.

SECTION 3.10

95 What is your personal view on testing and evaluation in relation to the observations in this section? What experience have you had of various policies in this area, and what do you yourself do or plan to do when it is necessary to assess your students?

96 Assess any other public examination format(s) that you have come into contact with in a similar way to my assessment of the Cambridge Certificate examinations.

97 How do you respond to Desmond Morris's suggestion that present-day public examinations are at least in part a version of tribal initiation rituals?

SECTION 3.11

98 If you were presented by the authority for which you worked as a language teacher with a rigid course plan or curriculum from which you were not free to deviate, what would you do in fact? Examine carefully the motives behind your answer(s).

99 Try to obtain some catalogues which exhibit the six-level arrangement of language-learning years. Consider this publishers' device in relation to institutional practices with which you are familiar, and try to decide whether the device is useful or not.

100 Discuss the two models that I have provided for the six-level plan, especially in relation to your experience of the way things are generally done. How does one find the balance between restrictive security (for both student and teacher) and open-ended freedom that might lead to anarchy?

Notes and references

The notes and references are organized according to the three parts of the book and in terms of the various sections within those parts. They will serve as:
1 a means of indicating sources to which I have gone or of which I have been aware while compiling my own material;
2 a means of helping students augment what is offered here, either within the framework of a course or for private study;
3 a guide to background material that can be used specifically in relation to project material in appendix 3 (or any similar project material).
I have, if anything, erred on the generous side: there is probably more source material here than most people will want or need in their coursework. One reason for this is the problem that source materials are not always easily available in different parts of the world: British books may be more easily obtainable than American (or vice versa), or for various reasons libraries may not have a comprehensive selection. I have therefore tried to provide enough titles so that some at least should be recoverable locally. Additionally, I have tried to provide a spread of titles over the last twenty years in particular, so that students may be able to compare changes of approach. To that end, each name listed in the notes is accompanied by the year of publication of the work concerned.

The titles referred to are almost entirely in English. They are by no means the only titles available that discuss the various topics mentioned. Others may be available to students, in English and in other languages, and should of course be consulted too, as the need arises.

Part 1: Linguists and language

Notes to section 1.0

1 The concept 'scientific method' is discussed in many works. Those which have particularly interested me are:
Bronowski 1977
Gregory 1981, ch. 8
Hesse 1967
Lyons 1981, pp. 40ff.
Magee 1973, esp. chs 2 and 3
Popper 1959/68 and 1963/72
2 The concept 'language as a tool' is discussed in:
Bronowski 1977, pp. 128f. and 150ff.
Gregory 1981, pp. 48ff.
Leakey 1981, ch. 8, esp. pp. 134ff.

3 Sources for further information about Ferdinand de Saussure, the 'father of modern linguistics', include:
Crystal 1971 (consult index)
Dinneen 1967, ch. 7
Lyons 1968, p. 38
Robins 1964/79 (consult index)
The 1978 Payot edition of de Saussure 1916 contains a detailed biographical critique in French by Tullio de Mauro.

Section 1.1

1 In this survey I have restricted the term 'linguistics' to a science that has developed mainly in the twentieth century. Not everyone, however, uses the term in this way. Ellegård and Hoenigswald, for example, treat 'linguistics' as a term for all organized language study ever undertaken. Following them, it is possible to talk about 'classical linguistics' (in ancient Greece and Rome) or 'medieval linguistics'. Chomsky refers to studies of philosophical grammar in France in the seventeenth and eighteenth centuries that follow the style of René Descartes as 'Cartesian linguistics'.
2 Works referring to the historical development of linguistics, philology and language study generally include:

Bynon 1977	Hoenigswald 1968
Crystal 1971	Jakobson 1973
de Saussure 1916	Kiparski 1970
Dinneen 1967	Lyons 1970b, 1976, 1981
Ellegård 1968	Robins 1951, 1964/79, 1967, 1976
Hill 1969	

3 Works which discuss science and myth include:
Freund 1965
Gregory 1981, part 1
Grimal 1965, introduction
Magee 1973, ch. 3
Popper 1963/72, esp. pp. 37f.
4 Works which discuss linguistics and social relativism include:
Boas 1911a and b, 1940
Fishman 1968, 1970
Hymes 1964
Lado 1957
Peñalosa 1981
Tyler 1969
Whorf 1956
5 Works which discuss linguistic science in relation to language teaching and learning include:

Abercrombie 1965	De Camp 1969
Allen & Corder 1973–7	Finocchiaro 1974
Bloomfield 1942	Fries 1945
Corder 1973	Halliday et al. 1964
Crystal 1971	Lado 1957, 1964

Robins 1964/79   Widdowson 1979
Strevens 1965, 1977   Wilkins 1972
Wardhaugh 1974
6 References to major schools of linguistics can be found in sections 1.20 and
  2.10, and in the works cited in note 2 above.
7 Manuals of linguistics and general works on language include:
  Aitchison 1978   Hill 1969
  Akmajian et al. 1979 Hockett 1958
  Bloomfield 1933   Lyons 1968, 1981
  Bolinger 1968   Peñalosa 1981
  Crystal 1971   Potter 1967
  de Saussure 1916   Sapir 1921
  Gleason 1955/61   Traugott & Pratt 1980
  Hall 1964
8 In the course of preparing this material for publication my attention was
  drawn to a recent survey entitled 'Some issues on which linguists can agree',
  by Richard Hudson of University College London, published in the *Journal
  of Linguistics*, 17 (1981), pp. 333–43. Some thirty British linguists were
  involved, and such a questionnaire-based survey could usefully be extended
  beyond the UK. The survey is a kind of catalogue of short points, and I am
  happy to note a considerable overlap between what his respondents say and
  what my own rather differently organized review contains. Interested readers
  should, however, make the comparison for themselves.

Section 1.2

1 Animal communication and biological aspects of language are discussed in:
  Bronowski 1977   Linden 1975/76
  Fisher 1982   Marshall 1970
  Griffin 1981   Peñalosa 1981
  Leakey 1981   Premack 1977
  Leakey & Lewin 1978 Rumbaugh 1977
  Lenneberg 1967   Sebeok 1977
  Lieberman 1975   Smith 1976
2 The container–continuum approach, as used from time to time in this study,
  is my own.
3 For brief discussions of the secondary nature of the human vocal–aural
  apparatus, see:
  Abercrombie 1967, pp. 20ff.
  O'Connor 1973, pp. 22ff.

Section 1.3

1 Studies dealing with child development, particularly in terms of the work of
  Jean Piaget, include:
  Beard 1969   Flavell 1963
  Boden 1980   Gorman 1972
  Donaldson 1978   Inhelder & Piaget 1958

Pearce 1977　　　　　　　　　Pulaski 1971
Piaget 1969/70, 1972/73　　　Travers 1977
Piaget & Inhelder 1969

2 Works relating to child language acquisition include:

Bellugi & Brown 1964　　　　Lyons 1981
Brown 1973　　　　　　　　　Macaulay 1980
Campbell & Wales 1970　　　McNeill 1970
Crystal 1976　　　　　　　　　Peñalosa 1981
Dale 1976　　　　　　　　　　Spolsky 1978
Elliot 1981　　　　　　　　　Stern 1969
Ferguson 1971　　　　　　　　Villiers & Villiers 1979
Fletcher & Garman 1979　　Weir 1962
Halliday 1975　　　　　　　　Wells 1981

3 Works relating to multi- and bilingualism include:

Aitken & McArthur 1979 (ref. esp. to Scotland)
Alatis 1972
Ferguson 1959/66
Ferguson & Heath 1981 (ref. esp. to the USA)
Fishman 1968, 1970
Halliday 1968
Hymes 1964
Lyons 1981
Mackey 1967, 1968
Peñalosa 1981
Robins 1976
Spolsky 1972, 1978
Spolsky & Cooper 1978
Weinreich 1953/74

4 Works which discuss the nature–nurture controversy and related matters (in psychology, ethology, linguistics, etc.) include:

Borger & Seaborne 1966 (theories of learning generally)
Chomsky 1967 (against behaviourism)
Fisher 1982 (reviewing the controversy: pp. 115ff.)
Griffin 1981 (ethologically: see index, nature–nurture)
Miller 1964 (psychological movements generally)
Peters 1968 (reviewing behaviourism)
Skinner 1953, 1957 (behaviourism)
Spolsky 1978 (general review)
Watson 1962 (behaviourism)
Wilson 1975 (sociobiology)

Section 1.4

1 The concept 'idiolect' is discussed in:

Lyons 1981, pp. 26f., pp. 268ff.
Robins 1964/79, p. 51

2 Ability, motivation, etc., in learning generally and in language learning in particular, are discussed in:

Borger & Seaborne 1966 (general)
Cole et al. 1972 (in relation to culture)
Finocchiaro 1974 (in language teaching and learning)
Lado 1964 (in language teaching and learning)
Miller 1964 (general)
Rivers 1972/76/83 (relating psychology and language teaching)
3 For a detailed historical study of language-teaching methods, etc., see Kelly 1969/76.
4 The opposition of the terms 'monastery' and 'marketplace' as used in this study is my own.
5 Studies relating to pidgins, creoles, trade jargons, etc., include:
Hymes 1971
Peñalosa 1981
Todd 1974
Traugott & Pratt 1980
Valdman 1977
Weinreich 1953/74

Section 1.5

1 Studies which discuss the arbitrariness of language symbols include:
Abercrombie 1967, pp. 11–13
Bolinger 1968, pp. 15f.
de Saussure 1916, pp. 100ff.
Dinneen 1967, p. 8
Lyons 1968, pp. 63f; 1981, pp. 19f.
2 Studies that discuss such matters as language loyalty, conflict, politics, planning, etc., include:
Peñalosa 1981
Sapir 1941/56
Traugott & Pratt 1980
Tyler 1969
Whorf 1956

Section 1.6

Studies relating to language, reality, worldviews, and the Sapir–Whorf Hypothesis (also sometimes known as the Whorfian Hypothesis and Whorfianism) include:

Black 1968
Boas 1911a and b, 1940
Dinneen 1967
Hymes 1964
Lyons 1981

Peñalosa 1981
Sapir 1941/56
Traugott & Pratt 1980
Tyler 1969
Whorf 1956

Section 1.7

For other discussions of what I am calling here the 'medium' and the 'message', see the works cited below. The expression 'medium' is current in linguistics generally, although it is not a central term (since much more attention is paid to speech than to writing). This use of 'message' as a linguistic technical term *may* be my own, as used here, but will certainly be immediately understood as I have used it.

Abercrombie 1967, ch. 1 ('medium' and 'language')
Lyons 1968, p. 54 ('double articulation', etc.); 1981, pp. 19ff. ('duality' in language)
Martinet 1960/64, pp. 13ff. ('double articulation')

Section 1.8

1 The terms 'phonic medium' for the medium of speech and 'graphic medium' for the medium of writing are not (yet) widely used, but would be immediately understood in any discussion among linguists.
2 For arguments relating to the primacy of the phonic medium in linguistics, see:
Bolinger 1968, pp. 12f.
Dinneen 1967, pp. 6f.
Lyons 1968, pp. 38ff; 1981, pp. 11ff.
3 Studies which discuss the nature of the phonic medium (speech), phonetics, phonology, the phoneme, language rhythm, etc., include:
Abercrombie 1965, 1967 (general)
Albrow 1968 (rhythm, esp of English)
Chomsky & Hallé 1968 (generative phonology)
Fudge 1970 (phonology)
Jones 1950 (the phoneme)
Ladefoged 1975, 1976 (general)
Laver 1970 (speech production)
O'Connor 1973 (general)
4 Studies which discuss the nature of the graphic medium (writing) include:

Abercrombie 1965	Diringer 1962, 1976
Barber 1964/72	Diringer & Freeman 1977
Bolinger 1968	Gelb 1952/63
Claiborne 1975	Jensen 1935/58/70

Section 1.9

1 For the concept 'articulatory set', see Honikman 1964.
2 Studies which discuss body language, personal space, social distance, paralanguage, kinesics and proxemics include:
Abercrombie 1956 (gesture), 1968 (paralanguage)
Argyle 1967, 1969, 1975 (general)
Birdwhistell 1952, 1970 (kinesics)
Bolinger 1968 (sound and gesture: pp. 13f.)
Fast 1970 (body language: informally)

Hall 1959, 1966 (general)
Hinde 1972 (nonverbal communication)
Morris 1977 (general)
Napier 1980 (gesture and the hand)
Peñalosa 1981 (paralanguage and kinesics: pp. 18f.)
Vygotsky 1962 (general)

Section 1.10

1 For some discussions of purism in relation to language, see:
Bolinger 1968, pp. 288f.
Lyons 1968, pp. 42f.
Peñalosa 1981, pp. 20f.
2 Studies which discuss the nature of language change include:

Aitchison 1981	Jespersen 1922
Bolinger 1968, chs 6, 7, 8	Lyons 1981, esp. ch. 6
Dinneen 1967, pp. 422f.	Martinet 1960/64, esp. ch. 6
Hoenigswald 1960	Sapir 1921
Hymes 1964, esp. part 8	

3 For 'interlanguage' in the sense of stages in learning and using languages
that demonstrate kinds of interference, especially in the satisfactory
acquisition of a new language, see:
Corder 1975b
Selinker 1972
Selinker & Lamendella 1981
Spolsky 1979

Section 1.11

Most introductory works on linguistics make brief references to equal
potentiality among languages, sometimes linking their remarks to sociocultural
relativism (see note 4, section 1.1) and the Sapir–Whorf Hypothesis (see the
note to section 1.6).

Section 1.12

1 For the specific discussion of language change as progress or deterioration,
see:
Aitchison 1981
Sapir 1921
2 For the original account of the terms 'synchronic' and 'diachronic', see de
Saussure 1916. For arguments in favour of the priority of synchronic
description, see Lyons 1968, pp. 45ff.; and 1981, pp. 54ff. For general
observations on the terms, see Dinneen 1967, pp. 199ff.; and Crystal 1971,
pp. 158ff.

Section 1.13

1 For a recent consideration of 'the fiction of homogeneity' in languages, see
Lyons 1981, pp. 24ff.

2 Works which discuss dialects, standards, special varieties of language used by social classes or professions (sometimes referred to as 'registers'), social attitudes towards language diversity, etc., are numerous. They include:
Aitken & McArthur 1979 (relating mainly to Scotland)
Benson & Greaves 1973 (general; less formal)
Bolinger 1968, ch. 9 (dialect)
Chambers & Trudgill 1980 (dialectology)
Ferguson 1959/66 (the concept of diglossia)
Ferguson & Heath 1981 (relating to the USA)
Guiraud 1971 (dialect & patois: France)
Hymes 1964 (general)
Ivič 1976 (general)
Labov 1972 (general)
McDavid 1969 (in the UK and USA)
Peñalosa 1981 (general)
Potter 1950/66 (for English)
Quirk 1962/68 (for English)
Robins 1964/79 (esp. pp. 50ff.: general)
Traugott & Pratt 1980 (esp. ch. 8: mainly English)
Williamson & Burke 1971 (in the USA)

Section 1.14

1 The classic discussion of languages in contact is Weinreich 1953/74.
2 For studies relating to creoles, pidgins, etc., see section 1.4, note 5.

Section 1.15

1 For Karl Popper's views on hypotheses, theorizing, science, falsifiability, etc., see:
Gregory 1981, pp. 249ff.
Lyons 1981, pp. 40ff.
Magee 1973
Popper 1959/68, 1963/72
2 For observations on Pāṇini and the Indian tradition of language study, see:
Dinneen 1967, p. 311
Lyons 1968, pp. 19f.
Robins 1964/79, pp. 377f.
3 For discussions of attempts at 'fixing' languages, see:
Crystal 1971, pp. 72ff.
Dinneen 1967, pp. 151ff.
Lyons 1968, pp. 42ff.
Palmer, F. 1971, pp. 13ff.
4 Works that use various models (usually presented in diagrammatic form) for describing aspects of language include:
Allen & Van Buren 1971 (Chomskyan linguistics)
Barber 1964/72 (language families)
Crystal 1971 (various)
Dinneen 1967 (various)

Halliday 1961 (language structure)
Halliday et al. 1964 (language structure)
Lyons 1970b (generative syntax)
Palmer, F. 1971 (various, mainly grammatical)
Robins 1964/79 (esp. linguistic comparison)

5 A complex and interesting general diagrammatic model of language that seeks to find a suitable place for lexis is provided by Nelson Francis in the introductory remarks on the English language in Webster's *New Collegiate Dictionary* (Merriam, Massachusetts, 1977), p. 24a.

Section 1.16

1 For two practical lexicographical attempts at handling social levels of language, styles of usage, etc., see the following works, both compiled with the foreign learner of English in mind:

Paul Procter, *Longman Dictionary of Contemporary English*, 1978
Tom McArthur, *Longman Lexicon of Contemporary English*, 1981

2 Works relating to sociolinguistics (the sociology of language, language ethnography, etc.) include:

Argyle 1969   Labov 1972
Bell 1976   Peñalosa 1981
Firth 1935   Pride 1970, 1971
Fishman 1968, 1970   Pride & Holmes 1972
Gumperz & Hymes 1972   Smith & Luce 1979
Hudson 1980   Smith & Shuy 1972
Hymes 1964, 1974/77   Trudgill 1974
Jespersen 1946

Section 1.17

1 Works relating to psycholinguistics (linking psychology and language) include:

Aitchison 1976   McNeill 1970
Carroll 1969   Pimsleur & Quinn 1971
Chomsky 1968   Rivers 1964, 1972/76/83
Clark & Clark 1977   Skinner 1957
Greene 1972   Slobin 1971
Jakobovits & Miron 1967

2 Works which discuss aspects of the brain, mind, consciousness, thought, neurology, and neurolinguistics, etc., include:

Akmajian et al. 1979   Fodor 1975
Bailey 1976   Gregory 1981
Black 1968   Griffin 1981
Blakemore 1977   Hampden-Turner 1981
Brown 1970   Kent 1981
Campbell 1977   Lyons 1981
Cole et al. 1972   Ornstein, R. E. 1975
De Bono 1967, 1969

3 Works which discuss computers, artificial intelligence, machines and language, etc., include:

Barr & Feigenbaum 1981   Minsky 1968
Boden 1977   Sloman 1978
Fodor 1975   Wilks 1972
Kent 1981   Winograd 1972

Section 1.18

Studies that discuss the various aspects of context include:
Bolinger 1968 (general)
Cole et al. 1972 (cultural)
Dinneen 1967 (general)
Firth 1935, 1951, 1957, 1964 (esp. situational)
Giglioli 1972 (social)
Lyons 1968 (general and in relation to semantics)
Traugott & Pratt 1980 (general)

Section 1.19

Many works discuss various aspects of the concept 'competence' (often linked with 'performance'). These include:
Bolinger 1968, p. 3 (basic)
Chomsky 1965a (originating the competence–performance concept)
Crystal 1971 (see index: general)
Dinneen 1967, pp. 358f. (on Chomsky's usage)
Hymes 1970 (communicative competence)
Lyons 1981, pp. 233ff. (on Chomsky's usage)
Munby 1978 (general review)
Palmer, F. 1971, pp. 151ff. (on Chomsky's usage)
Peñalosa 1981 (see index: on Chomsky's usage)
Traugott & Pratt 1980 (general review)

Section 1.20

1 For works which discuss the historical background to linguistics, philology, etc., see the references given in note 2, section 1.1.
2 For works which discuss the various schools and theories of linguistics and which provide overviews of controversial areas at the times of their publication, see the references given in note 7, section 1.1.

Part 2: Twenty-five centuries of grammar

(I had formulated the above title for this part before I was introduced to Louis Kelly's intriguing work *Twenty-Five Centuries of Language Teaching, 500 BC–1969*. Because of the variety of links, though not necessarily the identity of purpose and approach between this work and that, I decided to retain the resemblance.)

Section 2.0

1 The bibliographical background to the material in this and the other sections relating to the early history of the concept 'grammar' is not rich, at least as far as present-day linguistic works are concerned. This may be because of the synchronic emphasis that has been part of linguistics for most of this century, and possibly also because of a falling away of interest among language professionals in Europe's Greco-Roman inheritance. Be that as it may, a great deal of useful and relevant material can be found in encyclopaedias and historical works devoted to the periods, people and places mentioned. In particular, I would like to commend the fifteenth edition of the *Encyclopaedia Britannica* (Chicago 1976), which has a wide range of detailed articles on the classical and medieval periods, written by leading scholars in the various fields discussed.

2 Current works which seek to discuss, define and trace some part of the history of the concept 'grammar' include:
Dinneen 1967, esp. chs 3, 4, 5
Hamp 1976 (article on 'Grammar' in the *Britannica*)
Lyons 1968, part 1
Robins 1951, 1964/79, 1967, 1976 (article on 'Language' in the *Britannica*)

Section 2.1

1 Accounts of how writing developed in the ancient world include:
Claiborne 1975
Diringer 1962, 1976 (article on 'Alphabet' in the *Britannica*)
Diringer & Freeman 1977
Gelb 1952/63, 1976 (article on 'Writing' in the *Britannica*)
Jensen 1935/58/70

2 The term 'orature' as introduced here to contrast with 'literature' is my own.

Section 2.2

My various excursions into etymology can be compared with and augmented by (among others) the following sources:
1 in English: the etymological dictionaries of Chambers and Oxford (United Kingdom), Webster and Random House (United States); Onions 1966: *Oxford Dictionary of English Etymology*; Skeat 1882: *Concise Etymological Dictionary of the English Language*
2 in French: *Le Petit Robert* 1972; Larousse *Etymologique* 1971
3 Latin to English: Lewis & Short: Oxford, *Elementary Latin Dictionary*
4 Greek to English: Liddell & Scott: Oxford, *Greek–English Lexicon*

Section 2.3

1 The pairs *phýsis/nómos* and *analogía/anōmalía* are also discussed in:
Dinneen 1967, ch. 4
Lyons 1968, ch. 1
2 There are many works which discuss the place and importance of analogy in language and language learning. These include:
Barber 1964/72 (see glossary and pp. 65f.)
Bolinger 1968 (see index)
Dinneen 1967 (see index)
Kelly 1969/76 (see index)
Lyons 1968, 1981 (see indexes), 1976 (article on 'Linguistics' in the *Britannica*)
Potter 1950/66 (see index)

Section 2.4

Observations on Dionysius Thrax and Terentius Varro can be found in the following works, along with general discussions on the origin and nature of the parts of speech:
Dinneen 1967
Lyons 1968
Robins 1951, 1967

Section 2.6

Many traditional grammars of Latin and Greek contain short accounts of the model of cases falling away from an upright nominative. Both Dinneen 1967 and Lyons 1968 devote some time to the discussion of the concept of 'case' (see their indexes). A modern linguistic adaptation of case theory can be found in Fillmore 1968.

Section 2.7

1 A number of recent studies preface their remarks about modern grammatical theory with detailed references to 'traditional' approaches to grammar and language study, particularly emphasizing the impact of Latin models of grammar on the description of languages like English. These include:
Crystal 1971, ch. 2
Dinneen 1967, esp. ch. 5
Lyons 1968, part 1, ch. 2
Palmer, F. 1971, chs. 1, 2
2 The Scottish Classics Group has produced a set of reader/workbooks entitled *Ecce Romani*, first published in 1971 by Oliver & Boyd, Edinburgh, a division of the Longman Group.
3 *The Cambridge Latin Course* is also a set of reader/workbooks published by Cambridge University Press in 1973.

Section 2.8

The opposition between syntax and morphology is discussed in many studies, among them:
Dinneen 1967 (see index)
Hodge 1969
Lyons 1968, pp. 194ff.
Matthews 1970, 1974
Palmer, F. 1971 (see index)

Section 2.9

Paradigmatic and syntagmatic relations are discussed in many studies, among them:
Bolinger 1968, pp. 101f.
Crystal 1971, pp. 165f.
de Saussure 1916 pp. 170ff. (as paradigmatic and associative relations)
Dinneen 1967 (see index)
Lyons 1968, pp. 77ff.
Matthews 1974, pp. 155ff.
Robins 1964/79, pp. 47ff. (see also index)

Section 2.10

1 For studies that discuss purism, see the references given in note 1, section 1.10.
2 For studies that discuss dialects and standards, etc., see the references given in note 2, section 1.13.
3 For studies which relate to sociolinguistics, etc., see the references given in note 2, section 1.16.
4 Works which discuss applied linguistics include:
  Allen & Corder 1973–7
  Corder 1973, 1975a
  Lado 1957
  Lester 1970
  Politzer 1960
  Strevens 1965, 1977
  Wardhaugh 1974
  Wardhaugh & Brown 1977
  Widdowson 1979

Section 2.11

For works which discuss traditional, structuralist, transformational and other types of grammar, see the references given in note 7, section 1.1. Works to which the reader could proceed as a follow-up to the present material are:
1 initially:
  Crystal 1971

Lyons 1970b
Palmer, F. 1971
Turner 1973
2 for more theoretical developments:
Black 1968
Dinneen 1967
Hill, A. A. 1969
Lyons 1968, 1970a, 1976, 1977, 1981
3 for particular theories and schools of thought:
Bloomfield 1933
Chomsky 1957, 1965a and b, 1970, 1976
Firth 1951, 1957, 1964
Halliday 1961
Jespersen 1924, 1933

Part 3: The gift of tongues?

Sections 3.0 and 3.1

1 The list of publications relating to education and educational theory is vast. For a comprehensive review of the subject by a wide range of authors, see the fifteenth edition of the *Encyclopaedia Britannica* (1976), Macropaedia volume 6, under the following subject headings:
Education: economics of; history of; philosophy of; social aspects of; systems of; of the exceptional
2 Recent studies specifically seeking to discuss language, language teaching and education (all but two relating to the United States) include:
Ferguson & Heath 1981
Hawkins 1983
Lourie & Conklin 1978, esp. part 3
Spolsky 1972, 1978
Spolsky & Cooper 1978
Widdowson 1976

Section 3.2

1 The quantity of course materials nowadays available to language teachers is too vast and complex a matter to discuss here. No one can have readily available, make use of, or even know about, everything that is currently on the market (or that has been on the market not long ago, or may soon come on the market). A reasonably efficient approach for those who would like to have a well-stocked language teaching and learning centre has at least six aspects:
a) a main library area for materials currently in use or to be recommended for use on occasion
b) a nearby reference area for the fullest possible collection of teacher reference material

   c) a similarly nearby storage area for purchased and specially constructed aids of various kinds

   d) a well-maintained section for professional journals, special articles, conference reports, teachers' notes, etc., organized and catalogued as fully as possible

   e) a similar storage area for publishers' catalogues, price lists, locations of distributors, and other logistical information, also adequately organized, filed, and up-dated as necessary, with some kind of check kept on the mailing lists that interest the centre

   f) if possible, a 'museum' or archive section for copies of old, rare, unusual or otherwise special course materials for student-teachers to study

2 Works which are intended to educate teacher-trainees and help practising teachers include the following, with those aimed at English as a foreign or second language marked by an asterisk:

Abercrombie 1956	*Haycraft 1978
*Allen & Campbell 1972	Mackey 1965
Bennett 1968	Mathieu 1962
Billows 1961	Méras 1962
*Bright & McGregor 1970	Oinas 1960
Cornelius 1953	*Palmer, H. 1917/68
*Croft 1980	*Quirk & Smith 1959/64
*Dixson 1960	Rivers 1964, 1968, 1972, 1978
Finocchiaro 1964, *1974	Stevick 1957, 1982
*Frisby 1957	Valdman 1966
*Gatenby 1944	West 1960
*Gauntlett 1957	Widdowson 1971

3 Works which place their accent on the learner rather than the teacher include:

Brooks 1964	Oller & Richards 1973
Dakin 1973	Palmer, H. 1964
Finocchiaro & Bonomo 1973	Stevick 1976
Nida 1960	

4 For works which relate language teaching to linguistics, see the references given in note 5, section 1.1.

5 Studies which discuss attention and the concept of 'attention span' include:
Borger & Seaborne 1966 (see index)
Miller 1964, esp. ch. 4
Rivers 1972/76/83 (see index)
Walter & McCallum 1976

Section 3.3

For some views on teachers, students and materials, etc., see:
Altman 1972 (individualizing the classroom)
Born 1974 (student-centred programmes)
Rivers 1972/76/83 (teacher–student relations)

Section 3.4

1 For discussions of the nature of theorizing, see the references given in note 1, section 1.15.
2 For discussions of worldviews, etc., see the references given in notes to section 1.6.
3 For a comprehensive philosophical discussion of the concept of 'ideology', see Rejai 1973.

Section 3.5

1 For studies that discuss such topics as dialects, standard forms of a language, code-switching, bidialectalism, etc., see the references given in note 2, section 1.13.
2 Works which discuss pressures upon minorities to conform to national and other language norms include:
Lourie & Conklin 1978
Peñalosa 1981
Spolsky 1972, 1978
Spolsky & Cooper 1978

Section 3.6

For comprehensive consideration of the extended history of language teaching from classical times, see:
Dinneen 1967
Kelly 1969/76
Mackey 1965

Sections 3.7 and 3.8

1 For a concise discussion of the difference between a 'method' and an 'approach', see Strevens 1977.
2 For a detailed general consideration of recurring themes through 2,500 years of language teaching and learning, see Kelly 1969/76.
3 For a wide-ranging collection of specimen texts from authorities in language study and teaching throughout this century, together with extensive exercises and notes, compiled for the use of teacher-trainees, see Widdowson 1971.
4 For works which variously deal with aspects of methods and approaches discussed in these sections, see the references in note 2, section 3.2, as well as the following:
Alexander 1967 (introduction to teacher's book)
Bloomfield 1942 (on structuralism)
De Camp 1969 (on grammar–translation and structuralism)
Fries 1945 (on structuralism)
Jespersen 1904/61 (on direct methods, etc.)
Lado 1964 (on structuralism)
Mackey 1965 (general)

Osman 1965/67 (the Australian Situational Method)
Palmer, H. 1917/68 (direct/structural)
Sweet 1899/1964 (direct, etc.)
West 1941, 1960 (direct/structural)

5 For recent works specifically on communicative techniques and notional–functionalism, see:
Brumfit & Johnson 1979 (the communicative approach)
Johnson & Morrow 1981 (communication in the classroom)
Leech & Svartvik 1975 (a grammar of English)
Littlewood 1981 (communicative language teaching)
Munby 1978 (communicative syllabus design)
Van Ek & Alexander 1977 (notional–functionalism)
Widdowson 1978 (teaching language as communication)
Wilkins 1976 (notional syllabuses)

6 Works which discuss mechanical aids in language learning include:
Dakin 1973 (the language laboratory)
Grazia & Sohn 1964 (programmed learning)
Howatt 1969 (programmed learning)
Lado 1964, part 3 (general)
Marty 1960 (language laboratory), 1962 (programmed learning)
Ornstein, Ewton & Mueller 1970 (general)
Stack 1966 (language laboratory)

7 Works which discuss audiovisual aids generally include:
Corder 1966
Hirsch 1954
Huebener 1960
Lee & Coppen 1964
Wright 1976

8 Works which discuss theories of learning, especially in relation to education and/or the acquiring of languages, include:
Ausubel 1966 (cognitive educational psychology)
Belyayev 1964 (the psychology of teaching foreign languages)
Bigge 1971 (learning theories, and teaching)
Borger & Seaborne 1966 (the psychology of learning)
Edson 1975 (the nature of learning)
Hill 1963 (the psychology of learning)
Jakobovits & Miron 1967 (the psychology of language)
Pimsleur & Quinn 1971 (the psychology of second-language learning)
Rivers 1964 (psychology and foreign-language teaching)

9 I have avoided any discussion of such 'fringe' approaches to language teaching and learning as Gattegno's Silent Way and Lozanov's Suggestopedia. For descriptions of these, see Stevick 1976.

Section 3.9

1 Discussions on mistake-making (usually found in indexes under the word 'error') and attitudes to correction can be found in greater or less detail in most works on teaching. Typical of those in language-teaching works are:
Dakin 1973, pp. 14f.
Finocchiaro 1974, pp. 72f.
Rivers 1972/76/83 (see index)
2 Studies discussing error analysis include:
Corder 1967, 1973, 1975b
Richards 1974
Selinker 1972
Selinker & Lamendella 1981
Spolsky 1979

Section 3.10

1 Works relating to language testing include:
Davies 1968 · Oller 1979
Finocchiaro 1974 · Oller & Perkins 1978, 1979
Harris 1969 · Rivers 1972/76/83
Heaton 1975 · Upshur & Fata 1969
Lado 1964 · Valette 1967
2 Desmond Morris discusses examinations as initiation rites in *The Human Zoo* (1969).

Section 3.11

Sources of information on curriculum planning, syllabus design, etc., are many and varied, and often linked with the policies of specific educational systems. Three sources relating to the English language are:
Finocchiaro 1974
Haycraft 1978
Munby 1978

Select bibliography

I have tried to make the bibliography as comprehensive and as useful as possible for those who wish to pursue various areas of interest further, and/or to have some suggested sources to go to for research work, term papers and the like. The list is not, however, exhaustive; indeed, exhaustiveness nowadays is a virtual impossibility. Additionally, even a comprehensive selection is tinged to some extent by the preferences and special interests of the one who makes the selection. That is no doubt the case with this bibliography. It will serve, nonetheless, as a point of departure for newcomers to the various fields, and, along with the notes and references, may be useful to teacher-trainers in compiling their own lists of reference material.

Abercrombie, David. 1956. *Problems and Principles in Language Study*. London and New York: Longman
   1965. *Studies in Phonetics and Linguistics*. London and New York: Oxford University Press
   1967. *Elements of General Phonetics*. Edinburgh University Press; Chicago: Aldine
   1968. 'Paralanguage', *British Journal of Disorders of Communication*, vol. 3, no. 1
Abercrombie, David, Fry, D. B., MacCarthy, P. A. D., Scott, N. C. and Trim, J. L. M. (eds.). 1964. *In Honour of Daniel Jones*. London and New York: Longman
Aitchison, J. 1972/78. *Linguistics*. London: Teach Yourself Books
   1976. *The Articulate Mammal*. London: Hutchinson
   1981. *Language Change: Progress or Decay?* London: Fontana/Collins
Aitken, A. J. and McArthur, Tom (eds.). 1979. *Languages of Scotland*. Edinburgh: Chambers
Akmajian, A., Demers, R. A. and Harnish, R. M. 1979. *Linguistics: An Introduction to Language and Communication*. Cambridge, Mass., and London: MIT Press
Alatis, J. (ed.). 1972. *Bilingualism and Language Contact: Anthropological, Linguistic, Psychological, and Sociological Aspects*. New York: Appleton-Century-Crofts
Albrow, Kenneth H. 1968. *The Rhythm and Intonation of Spoken English*. London and New York: Longman
Alexander, L. G. 1967. *New Concept English* (series). London and New York: Longman
Allen, J. P. B. and Corder, S. Pit (eds.). 1973–7. *The Edinburgh Course in Applied Linguistics*. Vol. 1: *Readings for Applied Linguistics*. Vol. 2: *Papers in Applied Linguistics*. Vol. 3: *Techniques in Applied Linguistics*. Vol. 4: *Testing and Experimental Methods*. London and New York: Oxford University Press
Allen, J. P. B. and Van Buren, Paul. 1971. *Chomsky, Selected Readings*. London and New York: Oxford University Press

Allen, H. and Campbell, R. (eds.). 1972. *Teaching English as a Second Language: A Book of Readings*. New York: McGraw Hill

Altman, H. 1972. *Individualizing the Foreign Language Classroom*. Rowley, Mass.: Newbury House

Argyle, Michael. 1967. *The Psychology of Interpersonal Behaviour*. Harmondsworth and New York: Penguin
 1969. *Social Interaction*. London: Methuen
 1975. *Bodily Communication*. London: Methuen

Ausubel, D. 1966. *Educational Psychology: A Cognitive View*. New York: Holt, Rinehart & Winston

Bach, Emmon, and Harms, Robert (eds.). 1968. *Universals in Linguistic Theory*. New York: Holt, Rinehart & Winston

Bailey, Ronald H. 1976. *The Role of the Brain*. New York: Time-Life

Barber, C. L. 1964/72. *The Story of Language*. London: Pan Books (1964, revised 1972)

Barr, Avron and Feigenbaum, Edward A. 1981. *The Handbook of Artificial Intelligence*. Calif.: Wm Kaufmann Inc.

Beard, Ruth. 1969. *An Outline of Piaget's Developmental Psychology for Students and Teachers*. New York: Basic Books

Bell, R. T. 1976. *Sociolinguistics: Goals, Approaches and Problems*. London: Batsford

Bellugi, Ursula, and Brown, Roger (eds.). 1964. *The Acquisition of Language*. University of Chicago Press

Belyayev, B. L. 1964. *The Psychology of Teaching Foreign Languages*. New York: Macmillan

Bennett, W. A. 1968. *Aspects of Language and Language Teaching*. Cambridge and New York: Cambridge University Press

Benson, James D and Greaves, William S. 1973. *The Language People Really Use*. Agincourt: The Book Society of Canada

Bigge, Morris. 1971. *Learning Theories for Teachers*. New York: Harper & Row

Billows, F. L. 1961. *The Techniques of Language Teaching*. London and New York: Longman

Birdwhistell, R. L. 1952. *Introduction to Kinesics*. Louisville University Press
 1970. *Kinesics and Context: Essays on Body Motion Communication*. Philadelphia: University of Pennsylvania Press

Black, Max. 1968. *The Labyrinth of Language*. Harmondsworth and New York: Penguin

Blakemore, C. 1977. *Mechanics of the Mind*. Cambridge and New York: Cambridge University Press

Bloomfield, Leonard. 1933. *Language*. New York: Holt, Rinehart & Winston; London: George Allen & Unwin, 1934
 1942. *An Outline Guide for the Practical Study of Foreign Languages*. Baltimore: Special Publications of the Linguistic Society of America

Boas, Franz. 1911a. 'Linguistics and Ethnology', editorial introduction to the *Handbook of American Indian Languages*. Washington, D.C.: Smithsonian Institution. (Reprinted in Hymes 1964)
 1911b. *The Mind of Primitive Man*. New York: Macmillan
 1940. *Race, Language and Culture*. New York: Macmillan

Boden, M. A. 1977. *Artificial Intelligence and the Natural Man*. Hassocks, Sussex: Harvester; New York: Basic Books

1980. *Piaget*. London: Fontana/Collins; New York: Viking/Penguin

Bolinger, Dwight. 1968. *Aspects of Language*. New York: Harcourt, Brace & World

Borger, Robert and Seaborne, A. E. M. 1966. *The Psychology of Learning*. Harmondsworth and New York: Penguin

Born, Warren C. (ed.) 1974. *Toward Student-Centered Foreign-Language Programs: Reports of the 1974 Working Committees of the Northeast Conference on the Teaching of Foreign Languages*. New York: The Conference

Bright, J. A. and McGregor, G. 1970. *Teaching English as a Second Language*. London and New York: Longman

Bronowski, Jacob. 1977. *A Sense of the Future*. Cambridge, Mass. and London: MIT Press

Brooks, N. 1964. *Language and Language Learning*. New York: Harcourt Brace Jovanovich

Brown, Roger. 1970. *Social Psychology*. United States: Free Press

1973. *A First Language: The Early Stages*. Cambridge, Mass.: Harvard University Press

Brumfit, C. J. and Johnson, K. (eds.). 1979. *The Communicative Approach to Language Teaching*. London and New York: Oxford University Press

Bynon, T. 1977. *Historical Linguistics*. Cambridge and New York: Cambridge University Press

Byrne, Donn. 1976. *Teaching Oral English*. London and New York: Longman

Campbell, Robert. 1977. *The Enigma of Mind*. New York: Time-Life

Campbell, Robin and Wales, Roger. 1970. 'The Study of Language Acquisition' in Lyons 1970b

Carroll, John B. 1969. 'Linguistics and Psychology' in Hill 1969

Catford, J. C. 1959/64. 'The Teaching of English as a Foreign Language' in Quirk and Smith 1959/64

1969. 'J. R. Firth and British Linguistics' in Hill 1969

Chambers, J. K. 1975. *Canadian English: Origins and Structures*. Toronto and London: Methuen

Chambers, J. K. and Trudgill, P. 1980. *Dialectology*. Cambridge and New York: Cambridge University Press

Chomsky, Noam. 1957. *Syntactic Structures*. The Hague: Mouton

1965a. *Aspects of a Theory of Syntax*. Cambridge, Mass.: MIT Press

1965b. *Current Issues in Linguistic Theory*. The Hague: Mouton

1966. *Cartesian Linguistics*. New York and London: Harper & Row

1967. 'Review of Skinner's *Verbal Behavior*', in Jakobovits and Miron 1967

1968. 'Language and the Mind' *Psychology Today*, vol. 1

1970. 'Linguistic Theory' in Lester 1970

1976. *Reflections on Language*. New York: Pantheon Books; London: Fontana

Chomsky, Noam and Hallé, Maurice. 1968. *The Sound Pattern of English*. New York: Harper & Row

Claiborne, Robert. 1975. *The Birth of Writing*. New York: Time-Life

Clark, H. H. and Clark, E. V. 1977. *Psychology and Language: An Introduction to Psycholinguistics*. New York: Harcourt Brace Jovanovich

Cole, Michael, Gay, John, Glick, Joseph A. and Sharp, Donald W. 1972. *The Cultural Contexts of Learning and Thinking.* London: Methuen

Corder, S. Pit. 1966. *The Visual Element in Language Teaching.* London: Longman
1967. 'The Significance of Learners' Errors', *International Review of Applied Linguistics,* 5/2.3
1973. *Introducing Applied Linguistics.* Harmondsworth and New York: Penguin
1975a. 'Applied Linguistics and Language Teaching' in Allen and Corder 1973–7.
1975b. 'The Study of Interlanguage', *Proceedings of the Fourth International Congress of Applied Linguistics*

Cornelius, E. 1953. *Language Teaching: A Guide for Teachers of Foreign Languages.* New York: Thomas Crowell

Croft, Kenneth (ed.) 1980. *Readings on English as a Second Language.* Cambridge, Mass.: Winthrop

Crystal, David. 1971. *Linguistics.* Harmondsworth and New York: Penguin
1976. *Child Language Learning and Linguistics: An Overview for the Teaching and Therapeutic Professions.* London: Arnold

Dakin, Julian. 1973. *The Language Laboratory and Language Learning.* London and New York: Longman

Dale, P. S. 1976. *Language Development: Structure and Function.* New York and London: Holt, Rinehart & Winston

Davies, Alan. 1968. *Language Testing Symposium: A Psycholinguistic Approach.* London and New York: Oxford University Press

Dean, Leonard F., Gibson, Walker and Wilson, Kenneth G. (eds.). 1971. *The Play of Language.* London and New York: Oxford University Press

De Bono, Edward. 1967. *The Use of Lateral Thinking.* Harmondsworth and New York: Penguin
1969. *The Mechanism of Mind.* Harmondsworth and New York: Penguin

De Camp, David. 1969. 'Linguistics and Teaching Foreign Languages' in Hill 1969

De Saussure, Ferdinand. 1916. *Cours de linguistique générale,*(1) published by Charles Bally and Albert Sechehaye. Paris: Payot
(2) new critical edition prepared by Tullio de Mauro. Paris: Payot, 1978
(3) translated by Wade Baskin, as *Course in General Linguistics.* New York: Philosophical Library, 1959

Devereux, E. (ed.). 1962. *An Introduction to Visual Aids.* London: Matthews, Drew & Shelbourne

Dinneen, Francis P. 1967. *An Introduction to General Linguistics.* New York: Holt, Rinehart & Winston

Diringer, David. 1962. *Writing.* New York: Praeger
1976. 'Alphabet' in *Encyclopaedia Britannica,* fifteenth edition, Macropaedia 1. Chicago.

Diringer, David and Freeman, H. 1977. *History of the Alphabet.* London: Unwin Bros.

Dixson, R. J. 1960. *Practical Guide to the Teaching of English as a Foreign Language.* New York: Regents

Donaldson, Margaret. 1978. *Children's Minds.* London: Fontana/Collins

Edson, Lee. 1975. *How We Learn.* New York: Time-Life

Ellegård, Alvar. 1968. 'Study of Language' in *Dictionary of the History of Ideas: Studies of Selected Pivotal Ideas*, vol. 2. New York: Charles Scribner's Sons

Elliot, A. 1981. *Child Language*. Cambridge and New York: Cambridge University Press

Fast, Julius. 1970. *Body Language*. New York: Evans; Pocket Books, Simon & Schuster

Ferguson, Charles A. 1959/66. 'Diglossia', *Word*, 15 (reprinted in Hymes 1964 and Fishman 1968)

　1971 *Language Structure and Language Use* (selection and introduction by A. S. Dil) Calif.: Stanford University Press

Ferguson, Charles A. and Heath, Shirley Brice. 1981. *Language in the U.S.A.* Cambridge and New York: Cambridge University Press

Fillmore, Charles J. 1968. 'The Case for Case' in Bach and Harms 1968

Finocchiaro, Mary. 1964. *Teaching Children Foreign Languages*. New York: McGraw Hill

　1974. *English as a Second Language: From Theory to Practice*. New York: Regents

Finocchiaro, Mary and Bonomo, M. 1973. *The Foreign Language Learner*. New York: Regents

Firth, J. R. 1935. 'On Sociological Linguistics', extracted from J. R. Firth, *The Technique of Semantics*. London: Transactions of the Philological Society, pp. 36–72. (Reprinted in Firth 1951 and Hymes 1964)

　1951. *Papers in Linguistics, 1934–1951*. London: Oxford University Press

　1957. 'Synopsis of Linguistic Theory, 1930–1955' in *Studies in Linguistic Analysis*. Oxford: Philological Society & Basil Blackwell

　1964. *The Tongues of Men & Speech*. London and New York: Oxford University Press

Fisher, Helen E. 1982. *The Sex Contract: The Evolution of Human Behavior*. New York: William Morrow

Fishman, Joshua A. (ed.) 1968. *Readings in the Sociology of Language*. The Hague: Mouton

　1970. *Sociolinguistics: A Brief Introduction*. Rowley, Mass.: Newbury House

　1972. *Language and Nationalism: Two Integrative Essays*. Rowley, Mass.: Newbury House

Flavell, John. 1963. *The Developmental Psychology of Jean Piaget*. New York: Van Nostrand

Fletcher, Paul and Garman, Michael (eds.). 1979. *Language Acquisition*. Cambridge and New York: Cambridge University Press

Fodor, J. A. 1975. *The Language of Thought*. New York: Crowell; Hassocks, Sussex: Harvester

Freund, Philip. 1965. *Myths of Creation*. New York: Washington Square

Fries, Charles. 1945. *Teaching and Learning English as a Foreign Language*. Ann Arbor: University of Michigan Press

Frisby, A. 1957. *Teaching English: Notes and Comments on Teaching English Overseas*. London and New York: Longman

Fudge, E. C. 1970. 'Phonology' in Lyons 1970b

Garvin, Paul L. 1969. 'The Prague School of Linguistics' in Hill 1969

Gatenby, E. V. 1944. *English as a Second Language*. London and New York: Longman

Gauntlett, J. C. 1957. *Teaching English as a Foreign Language*. London: Macmillan

Gelb, I. J. 1952/63. *Von der Keilschrift zum Alphabet*. Stuttgart. Translated as *A Study of Writing: The Foundations of Grammatology*. Chicago University Press (revised, 1963)

    1976. 'Writing, forms of' in *Encyclopaedia Britannica*, fifteenth edition, Macropaedia 19. Chicago

Giglioli, P. P. (ed.). 1972. *Language and Social Context*. Harmondsworth and New York: Penguin

Girard, O. 1972. *Linguistics and Foreign Language Teaching*. London and New York: Longman

Gleason, H. A. 1955/61. *Introduction to Descriptive Linguistics*. New York: Holt Rinehart

Gorman, Richard. 1972. *Discovering Piaget: A Guide to Teachers*. Columbus, Ohio: Charles Merrill

Grazia, A. de and Sohn, O. (eds.). 1964. *Programs, Teachers and Machines*. New York: Bantam Books

Greene, Judith. 1972. *Psycholinguistics: Chomsky and Psychology*. Harmondsworth and New York: Penguin

Gregory, Richard L. 1981. *Mind in Science: A History of Explanations in Psychology and Physics*. Cambridge and New York: Cambridge University Press

Griffin, Donald R. 1981. *The Question of Animal Awareness: Evolutionary Continuity of Mental Experience*. US: Rockefeller University Press

Grimal, Pierre (ed.). 1965. *Larousse World Mythology*. Translated by Patricia Beardsworth. Paris: Librairie Larousse; London: Hamlyn; New Jersey: Chartwell Books

Guiraud, Pierre. 1971. *Patois et dialectes français*. Paris: Presses universitaires de France

Gumperz, J. J. and Hymes, Dell (eds.). 1970. *Directions in Sociolinguistics: The Ethnography of Communication*. New York: Holt, Rinehart & Winston

Hall, Edward T. 1959. *The Silent Language*. New York: Doubleday (Premier Books 1961)

    1966. *The Hidden Dimension*. New York: Doubleday

Hall, R. A. 1964. *Introductory Linguistics*. Philadelphia and New York: Chilton Books

Halliday, M. A. K. 1961. 'Categories of the Theory of Grammar', *Word*, vol. 17, no. 3. Also available as a Bobbs–Merrill Language & Linguistics Reprint, no. 36 (Indiana)

    1968. 'The Users and Uses of Language' in Fishman 1968

    1975. *Learning How to Mean: Explorations in the Development of Language*. London: Edward Arnold

Halliday, M. A. K., McIntosh, Angus and Strevens, Peter. 1964. *The Linguistic Sciences and Language Teaching*. London and New York: Longman

Hamp, Eric P. 1969. 'American Schools of Linguistics (Other than Generative-Transformational)' in Hill 1969

    1976. 'Grammar' in the *Encyclopaedia Britannica*, fifteenth edition, Macropaedia 8. Chicago

Hampden-Turner, Charles. 1981. *Maps of the Mind: Charts and Concepts of the Mind and its Labyrinths.* London: Mitchell Beazley; New York: Macmillan

Harris, D. 1969. *Testing English as a Second Language.* New York: McGraw Hill

Hawkins, Eric. 1983. *Modern Languages in the Curriculum.* Cambridge and New York: Cambridge University Press

Haycraft, John. 1978. *An Introduction to English Language Teaching.* London and New York: Longman, 1978

Heaton, J. B. 1975. *Writing English Language Tests.* London and New York: Longman

Hesse, Mary. 1967. 'Laws and Theories' in *The Encyclopedia of Philosophy*, ed. Paul Edwards, vols 3/4. New York: Macmillan; London: Collier-Macmillan

Hill, Archibald A. (ed.). 1969. *Linguistics Today.* New York: Basic Books

Hill, Winifred F. 1963. *Learning: A Survey of Psychological Interpretations.* London: Chandler (University Paperback, 1964)

Hinde, R. A. (ed.). 1972. *Non-Verbal Communication.* Cambridge and New York: Cambridge University Press

Hirsch, R. 1954. *Audio-Visual Aids in Language Teaching.* Washington D.C.: Georgetown University

Hockett, Charles. 1958. *A Course in Modern Linguistics.* New York: Macmillan

Hodge, Carleton T. 1969. 'Morphology and Syntax' in Hill 1969

Hoenigswald, Henry M. 1960. *Language Change and Linguistic Reconstruction.* Chicago University Press

1968. 'Linguistics' in *Dictionary of the History of Ideas.* New York: Charles Scribner's Sons

Honikman, B. 1964. 'Articulatory Settings' in Abercrombie et al. 1964

Howatt, A. 1969. *Programmed Learning and the Language Teacher.* London: Longman

Hudson, R. A. 1980. *Sociolinguistics.* Cambridge and New York: Cambridge University Press

Huebener, T. 1960. *Audio-Visual Techniques in Teaching Foreign Languages.* New York University Press

Hughes, A. and Trudgill, P. 1979. *English Accents and Dialects: An Introduction to Social and Regional Variation in British English.* London: Arnold

Hymes, Dell (ed.). 1964. *Language in Culture and Society: A Reader in Linguistics and Anthropology.* New York and London: Harper & Row

1970. 'On Communicative Competence' in Gumperz and Hymes 1970

(ed.). 1971. *Pidginization and Creolization of Languages.* Cambridge and New York: Cambridge University Press

1974/77. *Foundations in Sociolinguistics: an Ethnographic Approach.* Philadelphia University Press, 1974; London: Tavistock Publications, 1977

Inhelder, Barbel and Piaget, Jean. 1958. *The Growth of Logical Thinking from Childhood to Adolescence.* Translated by A. Parsons and S. Milgram. New York: Basic Books

Ivič, Pavle. 1976. 'Dialects' in the *Encyclopaedia Britannica*, fifteenth edition, Macropaedia 5, Chicago

Jakobovits, Leon A., and Miron, Murray S. (eds.). 1967. *Readings in the Psychology of Language.* Englewood Cliffs, N.J.: Prentice-Hall

Jakobson, Roman. 1973. *Main Trends in the Science of Language.* London: George Allen & Unwin

Jakobson, Roman and Hallé, Maurice. 1956. *Fundamentals of Language*. The Hague: Mouton

Jensen, Hans. 1935/58/70. *Die Schrift in Vergangenheit und Gegenwart*. VEB Deutscher Verlag der Wissenschaften, 1935; second edition, 1958. Translated as *Sign, Symbol and Script* by George Unwin. London: George Allen & Unwin, 1970

Jespersen, Otto. 1904/61. *How to Teach a Foreign Language*. Republished 1961. London: George Allen & Unwin

   1922. *Language, Its Nature, Development, and Origin*. London: George Allen & Unwin

   1924. *The Philosophy of Grammar*. London: George Allen & Unwin

   1933. *Essentials of English Grammar*. London: George Allen & Unwin; New York: Holt, Rinehart & Winston

   1946. *Mankind, Nation and Individual*. London: George Allen & Unwin

   1954. *A Modern English Grammar on Historical Principles*. London: George Allen & Unwin

Johnson, Keith and Morrow, Keith (eds.). 1981. *Communication in the Classroom: Applications and Methods for a Communicative Approach*. London and New York: Longman

Jones, Daniel. 1950. *The Phoneme: Its Nature and Use*. Cambridge and New York: Cambridge University Press

Kelly, L. G. 1969/76. *Twenty-five Centuries of Language Teaching*. Rowley, Mass.: Newbury House

Kent, Ernest W. 1981. *The Brains of Men and Machines*. New York: McGraw Hill

Kiparski, Paul. 1970. 'Historical linguistics' in Lyons 1970b

Labov, William. 1972. *Sociolinguistic Patterns*. Philadelphia University Press

Ladefoged, Peter. 1975. *A Course in Phonetics*. New York: Harcourt Brace Jovanovich

   1976. 'Phonetics' in the *Encyclopaedia Britannica*, fifteenth edition, Macropaedia 14. Chicago

Lado, Robert. 1957. *Linguistics Across Cultures: Applied Linguistics for Language Teachers*. Ann Arbor: University of Michigan Press

   1964. *Language Teaching: A Scientific Approach*. New York: McGraw Hill

   1965. *Language Testing*. New York: McGraw Hill

Laurin, Jacques. 1971. *Les verbes: la conjugaison rendue facile*. Montreal and Brussels: Les Editions de l'Homme

Laver, John. 1970. 'The production of speech' in Lyons 1970b

Leakey, Richard E. 1981. *The Making of Mankind*. New York: Dutton

Leakey, Richard E. and Lewin, Roger. 1978. *People of the Lake: Mankind and its Beginnings*. New York: Doubleday (Avon, 1979)

Lee, W. R. and Coppen, H. 1964. *Simple Audio-Visual Aids to Foreign Language Teaching*. London and New York: Oxford University Press

Leech, Geoffrey, and Svartvik, Jan. 1975. *A Communicative Grammar of English*. London and New York: Longman

Lenneberg, E. 1967. *Biological Foundations of Language*. New York: John Wiley

Lester, Mark (ed.). 1970. *Readings in Applied Transformational Grammar*. New York: Holt, Rinehart & Winston

Lieberman, P. 1975. *On the Origins of Language: An Introduction to the Evolution of Human Speech*. New York: Macmillan

Linden, E. 1975/76. *Apes, Man and Language*. New York: Dutton, 1975; Harmondsworth and New York: Penguin, 1976

Littlewood, William. 1981. *Communicative Language Teaching: An Introduction*. Cambridge and New York: Cambridge University Press

Lourie, Margaret A. and Conklin, Nancy Faires (eds.). 1978. *A Pluralistic Nation: The Language Issue in the United States*. Rowley, Mass.: Newbury House

Lyons, John. 1968. *Introduction to Theoretical Linguistics*. Cambridge and New York: Cambridge University Press

  1970a. *Chomsky*. London: Fontana/Collins

  (ed.). 1970b. *New Horizons in Linguistics*. Harmondsworth and New York: Penguin

  1976. 'Linguistics' in *Encyclopaedia Britannica*, fifteenth edition, Macropaedia 10. Chicago

  1977. *Semantics*. Cambridge and New York: Cambridge University Press

  1981. *Language and Linguistics, an Introduction*. Cambridge and New York: Cambridge University Press

McArthur, Tom. 1981. *Longman Lexicon of Contemporary English*. London and New York: Longman

Macaulay, Ronald. 1980. *Generally Speaking: How Children Learn Language*. Rowley, Mass.: Newbury House

McDavid, Raven I. 1969. 'Dialects: British and American Standard and Non-standard' in Hill 1969

Mackey, William Francis. 1965. *Language Teaching Analysis*. Bloomington: Indiana University Press. London and New York: Longman

  1967. *Bilingualism as a World Problem*. Montreal: Harvest House

  1968. 'The description of bilingualism' in Fishman 1968

McNeill, D. 1970. *The Acquisition of Language. The Study of Developmental Psycholinguistics*. New York: Harper & Row

Magee, Bryan. 1973. *Popper*. London: Fontana/Collins

Marshall, J. C. 1970. 'The biology of communication in man and animals' in Lyons 1970b

Martinet, André. 1960/64. *Eléments de linguistique générale*. Paris: Armand Colin. English translation, *Elements of General Linguistics*. London: Faber, 1964

Marty, F. L. 1960. *Language Laboratory Learning*. Wellesley, Mass.: Audio-Visual Publications

  1962. *Programming a Basic Foreign Language Course*. Virginia: Hollins College

Mathieu, G. (ed.). 1962. *Advances in the Teaching of Modern Languages*. London: Pergamon Press

Matthews, Peter H. 1970. 'Recent Developments in Morphology' in Lyons 1970b

  1974. *Morphology: An Introduction to the Theory of Word-Structure*. Cambridge and New York: Cambridge University Press

Méras, E. A. 1962. *A Language Teacher's Guide*. New York: Harper & Row

Miller, George A. 1964. *Psychology: The Science of Mental Life*. London: Hutchinson, 1964. Harmondsworth: Penguin, 1966

Minsky, M. L. (ed.). 1968. *Semantic Information Processing*. Cambridge, Mass.: MIT Press

Morris, Desmond. 1969. *The Human Zoo*. London: Jonathan Cape

  1977. *Manwatching: A Field Guide to Human Behaviour*. Lausanne: Elsevier; London: Jonathan Cape

Munby, John. 1978. *Communicative Syllabus Design*. Cambridge and New York: Cambridge University Press

Napier, John. 1980. *Hands*. New York: Pantheon Books

Nida, Eugene. 1960. *Learning a Foreign Language*. New York: Free Press

O'Connor, J. D. 1973. *Phonetics*. Harmondsworth and New York: Penguin

Oinas, F. J. 1960. *Language Teaching Today*. Bloomington, Indiana: Indiana University Press

Oller, John W. 1979. *Language Tests at School*. London and New York: Longman

Oller, John W. and Perkins, Kyle. 1978. *Language in Education: Testing the Tests*. Rowley, Mass.: Newbury House

1979. *Research in Language Testing*. Rowley, Mass.: Newbury House

Oller, John W. and Richards, Jack C. 1973. *Focus on the Learner: Pragmatic Perspectives for the Language Teacher*. Rowley, Mass.: Newbury House

Ornstein, J., Ewton, R. and Mueller, T. 1970. *Programmed Instruction and Educational Technology in Language Teaching*. Philadelphia, Pennsylvania: The Center for Curriculum Development Inc

Ornstein, Robert E. 1975. *The Psychology of Consciousness*. San Francisco: Freeman. Harmondsworth and New York: Penguin

Osman, Neile. 1965–67. *Situational English*, Teachers' Books 1–3. London and New York: Longman

Palmer, Frank. 1971. *Grammar*. Harmondsworth and New York: Penguin

Palmer, Harold. 1917/68. *The Scientific Study and Teaching of Language*. Originally published in 1917, republished London: Oxford University Press, 1968

1964. *Principles of Language Study*. London: Oxford University Press

Pearce, Joseph Chilton. 1977. *Magical Child*. New York: Dutton (Bantam, 1980)

Peñalosa, Fernando. 1981. *Introduction to the Sociology of Language*. Rowley, Mass.: Newbury House

Peters, R. S. 1968. 'Behaviorism' in *Dictionary of the History of Ideas*. New York: Charles Scribner's Sons

Piaget, Jean. 1969/70. *Psychologie et Pédagogie*. Paris: Denoël, 1969. Translated by Dereck Coltman as *Science of Education and the Psychology of the Child*. New York: Viking, 1970; Harmondsworth and New York: Penguin, 1977

1972/73. *Problèmes de psychologie génétique*. Paris: Denoël, 1972. Translated by Arnold Rosin as *The Child and Reality: Problems of Genetic Psychology*. New York: Viking, 1973; Harmondsworth and New York: Penguin, 1976

Piaget, Jean and Barbel Inhelder. 1969. *The Psychology of the Child*. New York: Basic Books

Pimsleur, Paul and Quinn, Terence (eds.). 1971. *The Psychology of Second Language Learning*. Cambridge and New York: Cambridge University Press

Politzer, Robert L. 1960. *Teaching French: An Introduction to Applied Linguistics*. London: Blaisdell & Ginn

Popper, Karl. 1934/59/68. *Logik der Forschung*. Vienna, 1934. Translated as *The Logic of Scientific Discovery*. London: Hutchinson, 1959 (revised, 1968)

1963/72. *Conjectures and Refutations: the Growth of Scientific Knowledge*. London: Routledge & Kegan Paul, 1963 (revised 1972)

1972. *Objective Knowledge: An Evolutionary Approach*. Oxford and New York: Oxford University Press

Potter, Simeon. 1950/66. *Our Language*. Harmondsworth and New York: Penguin, 1950 (revised, 1966)
  1967. *Modern Linguistics*. London and New York: Oxford University Press
Premack, D. 1977. *Intelligence in Ape and Man*. New York: Wiley
Pride, J. B. 1970. 'Sociolinguistics' in Lyons 1970b
  1971. *The Social Meaning of Language*. London and New York: Oxford University Press
Pride, J. B. and Holmes, J. (eds.). 1972. *Sociolinguistics*. Harmondsworth and New York: Penguin
Pulaski, Mary Ann Spencer. 1971. *Understanding Piaget: An Introduction to Children's Cognitive Development*. New York: Harper & Row
Quirk, Randolph. 1962/68. *The Use of English*. London and New York: Longman, 1962 (revised 1968)
Quirk, Randolph and Greenbaum, Sidney. 1973. *A University Grammar of English*. London and New York: Longman
Quirk, Randolph and Smith, A. H. (eds.). 1959/64. *The Teaching of English*. London: Secker & Warburg, 1959; reprinted, London and New York: Oxford University Press, 1964
Rejai, Mostafa. 1973. 'Ideology' in *Dictionary of the History of Ideas: Studies of Selected Pivotal Ideas*, vol. 2. New York: Charles Scribner's Sons
Richards, Jack C. (ed.). 1974. *Error Analysis: Perspectives on Second Language Acquisition*. London: Longman
Rivers, Wilga. 1964. *The Psychologist and the Foreign Language Teacher*. Chicago University Press
  1968. *Teaching Foreign-Language Skills*. Chicago University Press
  1972/76/83. *Speaking in Many Tongues: Essays in Foreign-Language Teaching*. Rowley, Mass.: Newbury House, 1972; expanded edition, 1976; third edition, Cambridge and New York: Cambridge University Press, 1983
  1978. *A Practical Guide to the Teaching of English as a Second or Foreign Language*. London and New York: Oxford University Press
Robins, R. H. 1951. *Ancient and Mediaeval Grammatical Theory in Europe*. London: Bell & Sons
  1964/79. *General Linguistics: An Introductory Survey*. London and New York: Longman, 1964; Indiana University Press, 1964; third Longman edition, 1979
  1967. 'Dionysius Thrax and the Western grammatical tradition'. London: *Transactions of the Philological Society*
  1976. 'Language' in the *Encyclopaedia Britannica*, fifteenth edition, Macropaedia 10. Chicago
Robinson, W. P. 1972. *Language and Social Behaviour*. Harmondsworth and New York: Penguin
Rossotti, Hazel. 1975. *Introducing Chemistry*. Harmondsworth and New York: Penguin
Rumbaugh, D. M. (ed.). 1977. *Language Learning by a Chimpanzee*. London and New York: Academic Press
Sapir, Edward. 1921. *Language: An Introduction to the Study of Speech*. New York: Harcourt, Brace & World
  1941/56. *Culture, Language and Personality*. Menasha, Wisconsin: Sapir Memorial Publication Fund, 1941. Reprinted, University of California Press, 1956
Schrödinger, Erwin. 1944. *What is Life?* Cambridge University Press

Sebeok, T. A. (ed.). 1977. *How Animals Communicate*. Bloomington: Indiana University Press

Selinker, Larry. 1972. 'Interlanguage', *International Review of Applied Linguistics*, 10/3, pp. 209–31

Selinker, Larry and Lamendella, John T. 1981. 'Updating the interlanguage hypothesis' in *Proceedings of the Fifth Congress of Applied Linguistics*, pp. 402–24.

Skinner, B. F. 1953. *Science and Human Behavior*. New York: Macmillan
  1957. *Verbal Behavior*. New York: Appleton
  1972/73. *Beyond Freedom and Dignity*. London: Jonathan Cape, 1972; Harmondsworth and New York: Penguin, 1973

Slobin, D. I. 1971. *Psycholinguistics*. Glenview, Ill.: Scott, Foresman

Sloman, A. 1978. *The Computer Revolution in Philosophy: Philosophy, Science and Models of Mind*. Hassocks, Sussex: Harvester; New York: Humanities Press

Smith, Elise and Luce, Louise Fiber (eds.). 1979. *Toward Internationalism: Readings in Cross-Cultural Communication*. Rowley, Mass.: Newbury House

Smith, D. and Shuy, R. 1972. *Sociolinguistics in Cross-Cultural Perspective*. Washington D.C.: Georgetown University Press

Smith, W. John. 1976. 'Communication, animal' in *Encyclopaedia Britannica*, fifteenth edition, Macropaedia 4. Chicago

Spolsky, Bernard (ed.). 1972. *The Language Education of Minority Children*. Rowley, Mass.: Newbury House
  1978. *Educational Linguistics*. Rowley, Mass.: Newbury House
  1979. 'Contrastive analysis, error analysis, interlanguage, and other useful fads', *Modern Language Journal*, 63/5–6, pp. 250–7

Spolsky, Bernard and Cooper, Robert L. (eds.). 1978. *Case Studies in Bilingual Education*. Rowley, Mass.: Newbury House

Stack, E. M. 1966. *The Language Laboratory and Modern Language Teaching*. London and New York: Oxford University Press

Stern, H. (ed.). 1969. *Languages and the Young Child*. London and New York: Oxford University Press

Stevick, Earl. 1957. *Helping People Learn English*. Nashville, Tenn.: Abington Press
  1976. *Memory, Meaning and Method: Some Psychological Perspectives on Language Learning*. Rowley, Mass.: Newbury House
  1982. *Teaching and Learning Languages*. Cambridge and New York: Cambridge University Press

Strevens, Peter. 1965. *Papers in Language and Language Teaching*. London and New York: Oxford University Press
  1977. *New Orientations in the Teaching of English*. London and New York: Oxford University Press

Sweet, Henry. 1899/1964. *The Practical Study of Languages*. London: Oxford University Press (first published in 1899)

Todd, L. 1974. *Pidgins and Creoles*. London: Routledge and Kegan Paul

Traugott, Elizabeth Closs and Pratt, Mary Louise. 1980. *Linguistics for Students of Literature*. New York and London: Harcourt Brace Jovanovich

Travers, J. F. 1977. *The Growing Child: Introduction to Child Development*. New York and London: John Wiley

Trudgill, P. 1974. *Sociolinguistics: An Introduction*. Harmondsworth and New York: Penguin
1975. *Accent, Dialect and the School*. London: Arnold
Turner, G. W. 1973. *Stylistics*. Harmondsworth and New York: Penguin
Tyler, Stephen A. (ed.). 1969. *Cognitive Anthropology*. New York and London: Holt, Rinehart & Winston
Upshur, J. and Fata, J. 1969. *Problems in Foreign Language Testing*. Ann Arbor, Mich.: University of Michigan
Valdman, A. 1966. *Trends in Language Teaching*. New York: McGraw Hill
(ed.). 1977. *Pidgin and Creole Linguistics*. Bloomington: Indiana University Press
Valette, R. 1967. *Modern Language Testing*. New York: Harcourt, Brace Jovanovich
Van Ek, J. and Alexander, L. G. 1977. *The Threshold Level for Modern Language Teaching in Schools*. London and New York: Longman
Villiers, P. A. de and Villiers, J. G. de. 1979. *Early Language*. London: Fontana/Collins
Vygotsky, L. S. 1962. *Thought and Language*, edited and translated by E. Hanfmann and G. Vaker. Cambridge, Mass.: MIT Press
Walter, W. G. and McCallum, W. C. 1976. 'Attention' in *Encyclopaedia Britannica*, fifteenth edition, Macropaedia 2. Chicago
Wardhaugh, Ronald. 1974. *Topics in Applied Linguistics*. Rowley, Mass.: Newbury House
Wardhaugh, Ronald and Brown, Douglas H. (eds.). 1977. *A Survey of Applied Linguistics*. Ann Arbor: University of Michigan Press
Watson, John B. 1962. *Behaviorism*. Chicago University Press
Weinreich, Uriel. 1953/74. *Languages in Contact: Findings and Problems*. New York: Linguistic Circle of New York, 1953; republished, the Hague: Mouton, 1974
Weir, Ruth. 1962. *Language in the Crib*. The Hague: Mouton
Wells, Gordon (ed.). 1981. *Learning Through Interaction: The Study of Language Development*. Cambridge and New York: Cambridge University Press
West, Michael. 1941. *Learning to Read a Foreign Language*. London: Longman
1960. *Teaching English in Difficult Circumstances: Teaching English as a Foreign Language*. London and New York: Longman
Whorf, Benjamin Lee. 1956. *Language, Thought and Reality (Selected Writings)*, edited by John B. Carroll. Cambridge, Mass.: MIT Press
Widdowson, H. G. 1971. *Language Teaching Texts*. London and New York: Oxford University Press
1976. *Language in Education*. London and New York: Oxford University Press
1978. *Teaching Language as Communication*. London and New York: Oxford University Press
1979. *Explorations in Applied Linguistics*. London and New York: Oxford University Press
Wilkins, D. A. 1972. *Linguistics in Language Teaching*. London: Edward Arnold
1976. *Notional Syllabuses*. London and New York: Oxford University Press
Wilks, Yorick A. 1972. *Grammar, Meaning and the Machine Analysis of Language*. London: Routledge & Kegan Paul

Select bibliography

Williamson, Juanita V. and Burke, Virginia M. 1971. *A Various Language: Perspectives on American Dialects.* New York and London: Holt, Rinehart & Winston

Wilson, E. O. 1075. *Sociobiology: The New Synthesis.* Cambridge, Mass.: Harvard University Press

Winograd, T. 1972. *Understanding Natural Language.* New York: Academic Press; Edinburgh University Press

Wright, Andrew. 1976. *Visual Materials for the Language Teacher.* London and New York: Longman

General Index

The index lists the main concepts, technical terms, persons and places mentioned in the text. It is organized according to the sections of the three parts, and *not* according to page numbers.